IN MY SHOES
Teen Reflections on Hope & the Future

Written by Students of
Omaha South High Magnet School

Foreword by Erin Gruwell

Produced by The Omaha Young Writers Project
Allison Rose Lopez, Director

Published by WriteLife
(An imprint of Boutique of Quality Books Publishing Company)
www.writelife.com

Printed in the United States of America

Cover design by Watie White
Photographs by Oliva Rodriguez
Poem "1,000 Miles" by Jesse Ortiz

Proceeds from this book will go to Omaha South High Magnet School to fund literary speakers and literacy initiatives.

978-1-60808-029-8 (p)
978-1-60808-138-7 (e)

First Edition

To all the students who don't know they
have a story the world needs to hear.

Please write. Please speak.
And speak until you are heard.

Three quarters of the miseries and misunderstandings in the world would finish if people were to put on the shoes of their adversaries and understand their points of view.

- Mahatma Gandhi

Never criticize a man until you've walked a mile in his moccasins.

- Native American proverb

If you lose hope, somehow you lose the vitality that keeps life moving, you lose that courage to be, that quality that helps you to go on in spite of all. And so today I still have a dream.

- Martin Luther King, Jr.

Collective judgment is the most dangerous thing we can do.

- Renée Firestone, Holocaust survivor, to the students at Omaha South High Magnet School, March 1, 2011

Contents

Foreword

by Erin Gruwell
Teacher of the Freedom Writers

Unlike Carrie Bradshaw's love affair with shoes in *Sex and the City*, I choose comfort over style. After all, I am a teacher, not a fashionista. It would be impractical to strut around a classroom wearing 5-inch Manolo Blahniks. So, when I discovered the perfect fusion of style and sneaker by Cole Haan and Nike Air, I chucked my sensible shoes for a sleek design. The peek-a-boo toe would show off my French pedicure, while the cushy, tennis shoe sole made me feel like I could run a marathon. The shoes were perfect—sleek, stylish and oh-so-comfortable. It was too good to be true.

When my mischievous Labrador, Beau, decided to treat my prized possession like a chew toy, I knew it really *was* too good to be true.

When I showed my mangled shoe to our trusty town cobbler, he winced. "Another one?"

"Yep, I'm afraid so!" I said, embarrassed that my dog had destroyed yet another shoe. "Do you think you can fix this one?"

He carefully examined the tattered stiletto and muttered, "It's worth a shot!"

The cobbler's zest for repairing my shoe mirrors the dedication and commitment of teachers and tutors who believe that every student deserves another chance to shine and that writing could give students a chance for a new beginning. Rather than just tossing them aside, these educators make it their mission to show struggling students how writing about their perspectives for *In My Shoes* could help heal the hopeless and give them a chance to start over.

When my students, the Freedom Writers, who are similar to the authors of *In My Shoes*, entered my classroom at the age of 14, I quickly discovered that they hated writing and they hated me. One of my disgruntled students wrote in her diary that I "probably own like 500 pairs of shoes." Although this student obviously didn't know how little teachers make (and that I was still paying off my student loans), her sweeping stereotype affirmed that she thought we were different. We looked different, we dressed different, and in her pubescent mind, we *were* different.

In my student's mind, my shoes were a status symbol, and because she was poor and couldn't afford designer duds, our shoes created a class divide. I thought about my own shoes when I was in high school. I had various shoes for various activities; cleats for soccer practice, running shoes for cross country, colorful Keds for cheerleading, and sandals for socializing. I had multiple shoes for multiple roles. My students did not. Their shoes were tattered, had holes in them, were hand-me-downs, or knock-offs of the latest designer trend.

Realizing that shoes were a status symbol, I introduced my students to a Holocaust Survivor who endured frostbite because she didn't have the right pair of shoes during the Death March. "And to this day," she told my students, "I covet shoes." And she did. She hoarded shoes, actually as a way of compensating for something she had lacked as a teen.

When she challenged my students to "walk in somebody else's shoes," they realized that like her, they too have a story. Everyone has a story. And even if it wasn't as traumatic as walking through the Polish countryside, everyone should tell their story.

And like my students, who would go on to write *The Freedom Writers Diary*, the dedicated students in Omaha embarked on a writing project, where they learned the importance of walking in another person's shoes.

Many students enter the classroom, feeling alone and like they are the only person in the world to have experienced life the way they have. Some students struggle academically and may be impacted by barriers such as gang involvement, homelessness, social isolation, bigotry or illness. Often the best new beginning happens when students find their voice and find a connection to others.

In this moving book, *In My Shoes*, one young person explains, "I felt alone and disoriented, not noticing all the people that were trying to help me. On those chilly December mornings, I hardly ever wanted to get out of bed … One teacher in particular was kind, sweet, and understanding to me. When I sat in front of her, she talked not like a teacher to a student, but like someone that cared about me."

Another student writes about his struggles, "As a kid growing up, I only have had one parent: my mom. So, the money has never really been there, and we have always lived paycheck to paycheck." Oftentimes, students have to overcome serious challenges at home, keeping school from being a priority.

Further still, you'll read about the choices these teens face from day to day, in the struggle to find their own voice. "I had two choices growing up: either pick up a gun and a rag or grab the needle. But for me, painting graffiti was my escape from all of that. I saw graffiti as a window – a window of opportunity and freedom." Much like the Freedom Writers, some of the students found in this book needed to learn how to make better choices, and writing about their experiences helped them find a new path to take.

For the Freedom Writers, as well as these courageous authors in Omaha, writing became a cathartic experience that allowed them to realize that they are much more similar than they are different.

Meanwhile, other stories celebrate the victory of overcoming challenges that life often presents: "Life has torn me apart, and yet I know my hope is still alive. I won't ever let my hope leave again. Without hope, I will not achieve." All students have a story, but only once they choose to share their stories will they find hope along the journey.

When I picked up my shoe from the cobbler, he smirked and said, "Here. It's better than new." And even though there were still a few of Beau's teeth marks embedded in the heel, the shoe slid onto my foot, perfectly. It fit. The cobbler saw something in my shoe and knew it could stand another chance.

Maybe that's what this writing program truly is—tutors, like faithful cobblers, giving worn souls not only a second chance but a chance to share their journey. The writing process has helped these young people patch their personal holes and tattered souls. And maybe, just like those repaired shoes, these budding authors are now better than new. *In My Shoes* not only gave these students a chance to tell their stories so others could walk in their shoes, but it let the reader walk in someone else's footsteps as well.

Introduction

by Allison Rose Lopez
Director, The Omaha Young Writers Project

I launched the Omaha Young Writers Project, which led to the writing of this book, to give 45 students a voice. *In My Shoes: Teen Reflections on Hope & The Future* is a collection of stories about American teenagers, their daily lives and their hopes for the future. In these essays, the students who are living these stories share them as try to figure out where their lives are going after high school.

The student authors are seniors at Omaha South High Magnet School, and the one thing they made clear from my very first meeting with them in their English classes is that they're tired of feeling judged and as if they aren't truly *seen*. What these kids want is safety. To not feel judged. To not be hurt. To feel comfortable moving forward. To feel supported, valued and respected. To know that they will have a place in the world and a fair shot at success.

Perhaps these sentiments are best portrayed in the following poem, written by one of our students long before the project began:

1,000 Miles
by Jesse Ortiz

Look into my eyes and judge me if you want
I don't care

Because to find someone willing to walk in your shoes

is rare

If I didn't write how I feel
the closet would be closed

And the sadness behind my clown mask
wouldn't be exposed

To walk in my shoes would be like feeling death on
your back

And you fight every day to make sure your life line don't
go flat

Every day the reaper puts me on trial
So before you judge me

Put on my shoes
And walk 1,000 miles

The Theme

Before my initial meeting with the students, they had already
chosen "hope" as the theme for the book. They soon found that
hope is not an easy topic to write about. It was especially challenging to some of the students who were low-hope, meaning
they had trouble looking into the future and imagining where
they wanted to go.

Hope is about envisioning the future, so we went in with the
goal of helping them achieve the goal they had set for themselves. We gently pushed them to think about their futures and

to name the details. We learned about their dreams and asked the hard follow-up questions: "Then what?" and "If that's where you want to go, how will you get there?"

The Process

The essays were written with the encouragement and coaching of 29 adult mentors from across the Omaha community. I recruited 28 other people who agreed that one-on-one adult attention can make a difference in the lives of kids, and we met with the students twice a week for six weeks in their school library. Our task was to help them figure out how to tell their stories. Our group included a poet, a psychologist, professional communicators, editors, journalists, novelists, an accountant, an environmental consultant, a statistician, an illustrator, a retired teacher, a college student who was returning to his high school alma mater, a middle school librarian who lived in the neighborhood and took personal leave from her school to join us, and more.

The students were nervous at the beginning. So were the mentors. The students were excited about writing a book, but once we got deep into the process, some of them were saying, "Wait a minute. I don't know if I want to do this." Because by then, they really understood what it meant to show up, give of themselves and put their truths down on a page for someone else to see. It was a big leap, and although nobody pushed them to write about what was painful in their lives, many of them took the risk of sharing the stories that define how they see their lives today.

As mentors, we listened and read and encouraged. Our questions often provoked students to explore who they are today and why. Once they started talking, they couldn't stop, and that's when things got exciting. They wanted to be known. What we brought was a group of caring, educated adults who were there to coach, ready to listen and were clearly not going to judge. Some were scared to tell their stories because they were painful, and it's scary to admit to the world that you've been hurt. In some cases, they had kept so much inside for so long, they were stuck.

But the students saw that their mentors didn't flinch. The mentors saw acceptance begin to transform the way the students spoke about themselves. We saw their stories evolve as they wrote and discussed them. Several began with a sense of shame or embarrassment and completed the project feeling proud of who they've become. It was exciting to watch these transformations; the act of constructing their narratives made them take stock of the past and clarify what they wanted in the future. And that library was filled with the buzz of laughter and conversation and discussions of the future, of life. It was a room filled with courage and beautiful moments of real, human connection.

The Guiding Philosophies

I must give credit to three guiding stars of this project, beginning with Ferial Pearson, our phenomenal partner teacher whose heart is as big as the world. Her commitment to social justice and mission of making every student feel like a respected human being made this book possible. Without the emotionally safe environment Ferial created in her classroom long before we arrived, none of these students would have taken so many risks in working with their mentors. We also took as inspiration the philosophy of the Freedom Writers, which is all about emotionally engaging students in a safe environment, as well as the philosophy of 826 Valencia, the magical writing center in San Francisco which honors the teacher as the guide for projects like this and pairs adults with students for one-on-one attention to a writing project.

I'm convinced that these teenagers are not unusual in their honesty and wisdom. They have insight into their previous bad decisions and the bratty attitudes of early adolescence and conflicts with their parents and why they might push people away. They are amazing survivors. Some of these kids have been hurt and have the guts to say so. After all of these months with them, I've wondered if the biggest thing that separates them from adults is that they *haven't* lost their nerve to speak the hard truths when invited to do so.

So please, join us in really listening to teenagers by starting with these pages. Read their stories and honor their courageous honesty. Read and know that when we slow down enough to really listen to what kids have to say, there is so much to hear.

Self-Discovery Through Art

"I started getting more opportunities and that just opened my mind to new things and showed me how far I can get with my talent."

Painfully Beautiful

Before I really started getting into painting canvases or walls, I was drawing a lot. So, I guess I can say I picked up some pretty good skills. I started selling paintings, and I loved knowing that one person was going to have that in their home. I just loved the idea of that, but after a while, I got introduced to tattooing. And that fascinated me way more because of the fact that I could tattoo someone and that person would be keeping that for the rest of their life—not just on their wall until someday it might end up in a basement somewhere. No. This stays on you forever, so I love that I can put a piece of my artwork on someone's body and know that they are keeping that with them everywhere they go. But to do that, which I would love as my future career, I will have to practice a lot and build up my confidence and self-esteem because at times, I am very insecure about my art. So I've got to make sure that I've got that down. I can make sure that when a client comes in to get something done, I can make them feel secure about getting a tattoo done by me.

One of the appealing things about it to me is that tattooing is something I love to do and at the same time, it is something that can be my future career. I've heard it said that if you find a job you love to do, you will never work a day in your life. In other words, if you like what your job is, it won't feel like work. Another advantage would be that every day I would be learning new techniques because every day would be a new tattoo on a different body part. Other things that would keep everyday a new experience would be: wiggly clients, scared clients, wrinkly clients, brave ones, thin or thick designs, some simple tattoos, complex ones, colorful ones, plain black and white ones. There would be many different things to keep it interesting and keep me learning every day.

Also another thing I've got to do to get into tattooing is meeting different artists to see the different point of views or the different outlooks they have on tattooing. One of the other things that I have to do is sharpen up my skills as much as I can now. Then, when I start tattooing, I can just practice more and more. Another thing I have to do is to get my diploma because I'll need that also, so I am going to be working on that, too. And since I started my twelfth grade year here at Omaha South High Magnet School, on my own time I have been working on this sketch book or portfolio of all my nice work so that when I am eighteen and have my diploma, I can show people my work and hope that they like it.

Basically, the bottom line is I enjoy doing art. I love it when someone owns a piece of mine. So what better way to do that than tattooing? That way, the person loves what they have on their body, and I love that they are going to keep it forever. So I hope that my future career is the one thing I love—tattooing. And, yes, I know that I am going to go through a lot of obstacles, like hearing a lot of criticism. But sometimes I think that's good for me, so that I'll know what I need to work on and perfect because I just don't want to be some other tattoo artist and make money off of it. I want to be that tattoo artist that people want to go back to for their next tattoo and the artist that they will recommend to other people. That's the kind of tattoo artist that I want to one day become. With me putting all my attention towards my artistic skills, I just cannot picture myself doing some type of other job. It has gotten me out of a lot of bad habits and heavy drug problems; my mind used to be stuck on the drugs that I was taking. My choice of drug was pills, and I was always worried that I wasn't going to have a pack of pills the next morning so I could get high. I always tried to make sure I had enough for the whole week. I was never thinking of drawing, and when I did draw, it was just impossible because I was high everyday. I was getting to the point where I was getting sick and tired that I wouldn't feel high after popping fifteen pills at once. And I got so overwhelmed by the amount of pills I was taking every week that I just had to let it all out. So I reached out for real help, but I got so let down. When I tried getting help for my problems, nothing happened. After that letdown, I told myself *I am not getting help from friends or professional help*, and I let go of the pills for about three days.

In those three days, without noticing, I was drawing a lot—like non-stop. I told myself that *maybe this is the way out of all my problems*, and so I went for it and just threw all my drugs away and got more into my art. Teachers started noticing me for my art. Then, I started getting more opportunities, and that just opened my mind to new things and showed me how far I can get with my talent. One of the experiences that got me really far was the Packasso Project, which helps graffiti writers to do more legal art and expand their artistic skills. A lot of teachers recommended me to the people in charge, so they called me down to a meeting and asked us if we wanted to help make up a name and start this project and see where it goes. We already liked the artist Picasso, and since we're the Packers, we came up with the Packasso Project. Now we actually have a bunch of people who want to be in it! We have painted a lot of walls and gone to conferences where we present who we are. It has helped me to be more outgoing because I actually have to sit in front of a big group and talk, which I have always been afraid of doing. We have been able to do business with people who want us to paint their walls. We talk to them and see what they want. My favorite wall was when we went to my principal's house and painted her basement walls. It was my favorite project because we weren't given a topic and could just paint what we wanted. I painted my nickname, "Cream," and everyone else painted either a character or words that she wanted, which were "Faith" and "Hope." It looked awesome.

So I am thankful that I went towards my art and didn't just fall back into the grave I was digging for myself. I really enjoy when people look at my artwork and I can see their reactions. Becoming a tattoo artist would be one of the best things that has ever happened to me, and I just can't wait for that feeling of accomplishing what I've always wanted to be. This journey, like a tattoo, has been painfully beautiful.

"I see it as a way to prove that I exist. That I've been somewhere."

Against the Wall

Head's spinning, feeling good, thinking life's great. Been painting all night, and no one can stop me. I'm a vandal; I destroy everything, even your building. Wait, who's that coming around the corner? I run, red and blue lights flashing behind me. Her hand on the trigger, yelling "Stop!" and "Taze them!" Never polite. My hands are twisted, and my wrist hurts. Light is in my face, and all I can think is: this isn't the first time. How is it going to end this time?

People wonder why I do what I do. There's no one reason. I see it as a way to prove that I exist. That I've *been* somewhere. It's also my stress reliever and a way, among other things, that I cope with things. That's why people search for gangs, because they see them as a family. Gangs look out for you and know what you're going through. You might think, why would "family" jump you? Because it's a way to break you, so that no one else can. I remember seeing myself looking up, faded and my "family" is beating me up. Blood in my mouth and my lips split open. And all I wonder is how eleven seconds can seem to last a lifetime. I see now all of this happens because of a lack of hope. Everyone's looking for it. You try follow, searching like everyone else, but I'd rather lead and not be just an affiliation. I'm not affiliated, but if not for gangs, I wouldn't be here.

My grandfather was a strong and well-respected man. Unfortunately, I had to wait until he passed for me to see that. At his funeral, I saw people I've never even met before, telling me stories of a man I knew, but never in the way they did. He got into trouble as a teenager, too. He unfortunately was in a gang in East Los Angeles—White Fence, one of those old-school gangs. Somehow, he messed up and was given the choice of either jail time or the service. He chose the Air Force, later switching to the National Guard, and was sent off to Offutt Air Force Base. He was put in a group called "the un-trainables." It was a group for youngsters who, because of their background and troubled past, were considered un-trainable. A little time passed, and he met my grandmother, who whipped him into shape. Because he was a natural-born leader, men looked at him with loyalty and respect. He influenced and shaped many people who honored him at his funeral.

My grandfather also had a big influence within my family. For example, my cousin Fred D., as a teenager, also got involved with gangs, as did most of my family. All of them banged for Lomas. Fred D. and his brother and sister had had no place to go. As warm hearted as my grandfather was, he took Fred D. and the other two in. Fred D. told me how they used to talk before school about grades, girls, etc. Fred D., however, still ended up in trouble, and he did time for some gun charges. When he got out, it took him about two months to come and talk to my grandfather, his uncle. My grandpa asked what had taken him so long to see him. Fred D. said he was scared and didn't want to get yelled at. My grandpa asked Fred D. why he wasn't afraid of people with guns but was afraid of his own uncle and also if he thought of himself as a man. And Fred D. had to think about it for a while and replied, "No. But uncle, I've finished my GED and got accepted to UNO." And my grandfather just smiled. He knew Fred D. was scared to talk to him, but that fear and respect made him set his life straight. That's one example of how a bad decision may lead to a good one.

And how did I come to all my bad decisions? I first noticed a change in myself when my Uncle Bob died. The year before he died is when I got very close to him. On April 20, 2009, when he found out I smoked bud, he let me in on his *business*. Yeah, my uncle helped a lot of people, but everyone does something wrong or illegal in life. He taught me a lot about both of his very different businesses. Losing him was like losing a father. The thing I remember most when he died was going to the hospital thinking he was still alive and walking into that room, looking at him, wondering why none of the machines were hooked up to him. And that's when my mother told me that he had died. He was young, and it made me realize that life can end at any time.

About this time is when I started getting caught up in just dumb-ass things—shoplifting, graffiti, getting caught with weed, and even being under investigation for robbery, which led to my door being kicked down by police and having my room searched. *And here I am now, handcuffed against the wall for graffiti again.*

This isn't the end of my story; this is what made me change. I needed to change my life, stop stealing, robbing, selling drugs, graffiti, all this needed to stop. The Packasso Project, a program which helps ex-graffiti artists get off the streets, was there for me. And it's a way to show everyone I *want* to change. I have permission walls now to express my art, and I feel I'm going somewhere. These people are helping me explore my artistic ability while showing that graffiti can be harmless and an art form. I'm showing the courts that I'm on a good track and will soon graduate. I'm not sure where I'll be in the next ten years, but I know it's not where I *was* headed, but I'll be doing what I love. I love you, Grandpa, and I miss you and Uncle Bob very much. This was for you.

"In almost all ways, art has made me who I am."

Art Therapy

Art, a journey that will never end, through the eyes of others. Keeping them from knowing what is the next creation. Art has hit me like concrete and is forever stuck in me. It is my escape. Unlike others who drink or do drugs, art is my drug of choice. It has filled my life with something productive and taught me to think clearly. It has made my outlook on life come to life. Art's presence in my life started long before I had even realized it.

When I was seven or eight, I got my first Lego set. If I could've been just building all day back then, I would never be bored. It was almost like an escape for me, to just be myself and let nobody tell me different. Whether it had instructions or not, I would build anyway. I used to make my own versions of spacecrafts. Sometimes, it was castles or even miniature houses. As long as I was creating something, I was content. Staying up way past midnight, I remember my mom saying, "Put those things away. It's too late!" That was probably the beginning stages of my creativity and focus.

A few years later, I spent my free time taking apart electronics like radios, VCRs, clocks, and my Playstation 2. (Let's just say the Playstation didn't make it.) Electronics just seemed to amaze me. I guess that I just wanted to strip the things down to their main components to see how they worked and how they all came together to make them work. Piecing them back together seemed to be the most difficult. I didn't have any idea what I was doing, but it seemed to intrigue me. Little did I know, I was laying the framework of my creativity.

Then, high school came around. I wasn't the most highly motivated student. Freshman year, I had thirty-two absences in my last hour alone. (It happened to be gym, and the teacher wasn't so great. I really should've stayed anyways.) At that time, I was in just one art class called Exploratory Art. I remember one project. We had to make a composition with a close-up picture of something. Mine happened to be of a paint splatter. I made tons of big and small dots with a lot of random colors. When I think about it now, it was the most boring and vague class that the art department had. It had painting, drawing, oil pastels, and some clay. But it was just introductory and wasn't in-depth. However, that was my kickoff. My drawing and painting carried over to my home life.

Painting was like getting a brand new Lego set to do with what I pleased, except painting allowed me to be more abstract and create freely. Painting for me is expressing my feelings through colors, and it gives me a better vision of what I was trying and am still trying to create. Once again, I found myself spending countless hours at night (a little quieter) being myself and escaping reality.

At the same time, school became more bearable. Having that art class gave me incentive, and I was always wanting something better. Some of the classes were: Intro to Studio, Studio Art, Figure Drawing, and finally, Metal Smith. Metal Smith has opened a new door in my imagination. Looking back now, taking all those electronics apart helped me to see how things were put together and actually helped me to understand and create a puzzle of mastery.

I just filled in all my cracks with art, and it helped me to stay in school. It gave me structure, and it was my hard place to stay forever. After that year, I was like a train, and I couldn't help but to make more and more art. It has made my life enjoyable, and I now have something to look forward to one day. I hope that soon it will take me far beyond my expectations.

I am currently creating jewelry and have put my Metal

Smith class to good use. I hope to soon have a selling party and save up money to get me to the right people or anything, really. I've made some sculptures with winding wire and by tying and stamping various items together. I cannot wait to see where I end up in the future. Hopefully, I'll become noticed for my accomplishments.

In almost all ways, art has made me who I am. Art as a whole was my therapist. I couldn't imagine dedicating myself to anything else as much as I do art. I sometimes wish I could've started when I was much younger, to be the new-age DaVinci. Art has been a journey for me, and I have only scratched the surface. It is a changing game that has endless possibilities. It is finally my turn to show people the things that I can create. I hope one day that I will become a well-known artist and know countless people all over the world.

"I'm saying art has saved my life and will continue to do so."

My Name is Famous But My Face is Unknown

Art is a really big part of my life. It changed my life in a big way—in a good way and a bad way. I first found art when I was a freshman in high school, but it wasn't art in general. It was graffiti. And I knew from that point on, one day, one way or another, I was going to be somebody. To a lot of people, art may just be a hobby they have on the side, but to me, it's not just a simple hobby that I have on the side. To me, it's life. In the beginning, I was pretty much just on a warpath for destruction. On a path to be a well-known vandal. Later in life, I found a better path in the form of art. And by that, I'm saying art has saved my life and will continue to do so.

In my freshman year of high school, I was pretty much lost in life. Growing up, I was always around some bad people. I had two choices growing up: either pick up a gun and a rag or grab the needle. But for me, painting graffiti was my escape from all of that. I saw graffiti as a window—a window of opportunity and freedom. I could climb out this window from the life I was living at home and jump into a whole other dimension. It's like when I jumped out that window and picked up my cans of paint, I felt careless and free. Like I was unstoppable. I went by a different name, I hid in the shadows, and I crept on the rooftops. It's just a whole other indescribable feeling that almost nobody understands. I would walk back through my neighborhood, and all the guys on the block were like, "Hey, yo, why you got paint on your hands?" and "Why don't you go slang this rock?" and "Why you wasting time painting? Come make some real money." But me, I was different. I didn't want all that. All I wanted was my name to shine, my name to be famous but my face to remain unknown in the eye of the man.

Once I got to Omaha South High School, I met a big group of kids. Some of the kids were my age, and some were older. All of these kids that I met that year were all graffiti artists in the south Omaha community. I looked up to all the kids who were older and introducing me into the game. Of course, they were all better than me, so all I ever heard was, "Man, you're a toy." and "You suck. Do you even try?" and "Give it up, man, you'll never be any good." All those words that might seem hurtful to a lot of people, but a young graffiti artist who is new to the game takes those words in the right way.

They never told those things to me to put me down; it was only encouragement. After months went by, I joined a crew, and every day and night I was doing graffiti, whether it be in school or out. No matter where I was, I always had to write on something just to get my name up. I wasn't shooting for the typical 15 minutes of fame. What I wanted was 15 decades of fame. I got my name up everywhere! I started gaining respect from the much older and much better crews. Next thing I knew, I was on top of the game. One of the most known unknowns, I was one of the greatest in the city. I would spend days at a time focused on graffiti. I would spend all morning racking my paint and collecting supplies. Nothing was ever paid for. After collecting our supplies, we would hit the train yards and spend our whole day there smashing 40s and burning blunts. By the time nightfall came around, we would creep down the streets and bomb (aka tagging) everything in sight.

For a long time, I was going down the wrong path with the wrong crowd. I was never caught for graffiti, but I was really starting to not care for anything else but graffiti. I started skipping class, not going to school, getting bad grades. And there was a moment in time where I thought I hit rock bottom in life. I was still writing a whole lot, and I came to find myself in a big hole. And I was only digging deeper.

By my junior year in high school, I started to run with one of the best crews in the city. So I had to prove myself to these guys. I was stepping my game up and hitting the bigger spots— the billboards, the freeway, the freeway signs, rooftops, hitting places on busy streets. My name then became one of the most famous names in the city. I was hearing it from kids, grown-ups, cops, teachers, the news, and even the teachers at school. There was times were even my own mother would ask me about my name. I then gained the respect from all my crew members and other crews. I was hated by society, cops, teachers and was just an eyesore to the community in general. At that point I really didn't care what people thought about me. I adored all the attention and had all the haters on my case about how I'm destroying my home, my own city. People told me I was hurting the people close to me because of the way I lived my life, like a rebel who did not care about anything but graffiti.

As time kept going by, I began to realize more and more about myself and what I was really doing with my life. I saw myself going down the wrong path, and I wanted to change that. I was still tagging and hanging around the same people, but I was never the same after I realized what I was actually into. I knew somehow, some way, that I had to pull myself out of that hole I dug for myself. I was slowly progressing the change on myself. I knew I did very bad my junior year in high school. Then, the end of the summer came, and school was starting. The school knew I was tagging in and outside of the building. A few years back, the school had come up with this program called The Packasso Project. Once senior year started, I had a really good feeling about this school year. The second day of school that year I was sitting in my third hour class and a teacher who I've never met before came and pulled me out of my class.

She began explaining to me what the Packasso Project was. The Packasso Project was that hand that I needed in my life to pull me out of my hole. Packasso was a program for kids who have been tagging and pretty much going down the wrong path. It was a graffiti art program where you were given all of your supplies for free. They got us legal commission work on local businesses around town. But before I could even join the program I had to complete a week of perfect attendance and the biggest most important part of the deal was *no more tagging*. If I wasn't going to stop my skipping or drop my old habits, she was not going to accept me. She gave me a day to think about it, and I did. I realized that the tagging wasn't the life I wanted; I wanted to do better in and outside of school. That was the day I turned my life around and got redirected onto the right path. I joined Packasso, and once I did, a lot of things changed for me in my life. Ever since I joined the Packasso Project, I've been on the right path. I'm no longer skipping any classes, I'm passing all my classes, and most important one of all, I was no longer tagging. I found other forms of art that I could master. Even though graffiti art is still my specialty, I have other styles of art to fall back on. I am now very happy in life. I've made a lot of new friends and met a lot of important people. I was inspiring to a lot of young kids that I saw going down that wrong path just like I was, but I was able to pull them out because they saw the progress that I was making in my life. I was getting legal walls, free supplies, selling canvases, and all sorts of stuff that's good. And because of that, a lot of young kids look up to me and say, "I want to be like you someday." To me, that's better than the 15 minutes of fame I got catching a tag on a dumpster in some alley. My life has completely turned around, and in the same way that I was going down the wrong path, it's because of art.

That's where I go back to my beginning statement; art has

saved my life and will continue to do so. Well, I have told you my story of my history with graffiti. There is hope in our community. All these kids need nowadays is a good role model to push them in the right direction in life. That's all it took for me, and now my life is completely turned around and I am on the right path for a bright future and a new beginning.

Learning Through Sports

"The crowd sounded like thunder. They were going crazy."

Unstoppable

Soccer has always been in my blood. My mom used to say my uncle was a soccer prodigy. She said he was good enough to go pro. Maybe if I work hard enough and have the passion he had, I could pick up where he left off.

My first heart-pumping experience with soccer was in 2006. I was 13 years old. It was my first game with my club team. I always knew I was fast, so I had a feeling as soon as I had the ball at my feet that something was going to happen. It was ten minutes before the first half was over. Coach put me in the game. I got the ball, and I juked two players. I was right in front of the goal. I kicked the ball. It flew like a bullet and landed in the back of the net. I felt like my heart was pumping out of my chest. I felt unstoppable.

That next year, my team, Viva Esperanza, made it to State Cup Semifinals. We were playing Arsenal. The score was 1-0, and we were down. The first half was almost over. It was really windy and cold that day—horrible conditions to play soccer. My friend Ruben had the ball. I asked for it, and he passed it to me. When I received the ball, I was outside the eighteen. I turned, and all I saw and heard was the net and Ruben screaming, "Shoot it! Shoot it!" I bent my left leg back, and with the top of my shoelaces, I hit the ball. The ball was in the air. I closed my eyes because I am not a left footer, and I was scared I was going to miss. When I opened them, everyone was running toward me and hugging me. I had scored a goal!

That next year, my high school soccer team, the Packers, made it to State Finals. It was the first time in school history that the Packers made it to the Finals. Everyone knew about it. It was all over the school walls. It was even on the radio. The announcers were saying in Spanish: *Vegan a apoyar a la escuela South High.*

The whole South Omaha Community was cheering us on. The team we were against was Lincoln East, and they were undefeated. They had a perfect season. Only four teams in Nebraska history had ever made it to State Final undefeated.

The game was at 7 p.m. When the game started, I felt like I was a professional playing in front of thousands of fans. Everyone's eyes were looking at us, and there were reporters everywhere. Cameras were flashing. When it was time to walk down to the field, I felt shivers down my spine. Fifteen minutes into the game we scored, and we were up, one to zero. We are a team that usually scores early and has a great defense. With our record-setting goalie, we don't get scored on a lot.

Ten minutes after we scored, the unthinkable happened; they scored on us. The first half was over, and the score was tied one to one. When the second half started, we were really pumped up. We knew we wanted it more. The game was intense. We were back and forth shooting at each other's goals.

Thirty-five minutes in, Lincoln East scored. We felt like we had been stabbed in our hearts. But that did not get us down. We kept going strong. There was forty seconds left in the game, and we had a corner kick. We kicked it, and out of nowhere the ball was in the back of the net. The crowd sounded like thunder. They were going crazy.

The regular game had finished, and it was tied so we had to go to extra time. It was the State Championship, so there had to be a champion. That's why we went to extra time. The first extra time went smoothly. No one scored. The second half of extra time was the most intense thing I have ever been through. Five minutes before it was over, they scored on us. The game was three to two. Then there was a minute left. We fouled one of their players in the penalty box, so they had a penalty kick. Lincoln East scored the penalty kick. The game was now four to two. Right after the penalty kick, the referee blew the whistle, and the game was over.

We had lost the championship game four to two, but that wasn't the worst thing. I was trying to see a recap of the game on the news later, and instead of that, they were showing what had happened after the game. A few of the Lincoln East students had ran down to the field and had thrown green cards up into the air, trying to say that we were illegals. I had been sad the whole day because we had lost the game, but when I saw that on the news, my sadness turned to anger. I couldn't believe that people would do such thing. I felt disrespected. I never disrespected them, so I didn't know why they would think it was ok to do such a thing.

"My teammates gave me the ball, and to me, that meant they trusted me and they knew that I would score."

Hope is Basketball

Before basketball, I was not a regular kid. I had no friends. I was always weird, and no one liked me. Now that I play basketball, I am goofy, funny and outgoing and also finding what I love to do. Playing basketball made me who I am now. I look forward to the future, where I will have a lot of things accomplished. I will go to college and be in the pros. To other people, basketball is just a game, but to me it's HOPE. It will give me freedom, happiness and wealth.

Coming from Sudan, the poorest country in the world, we had nothing to do except learn how to survive. I was not a regular kid because I wasn't wearing good clothing. Back home, we had no sports, no TV, no school, no music, and the list goes on and on. I can say I lived a rough life in that time.

When I was six years old, we decided to move to the U.S. to get a better life, and things were different. We moved to Houston, Texas, in 1998. There, we went to school for free and learned English, had a house, my mom got a good job, and we started living the American life. Unfortunately, my dad didn't come with us, which was the worst part of our trip to the U.S. He had to stay back home in Sudan to take care of our family who were left behind. It was me, my mom, my sister and brother.

I didn't play basketball at that time because nobody taught me how to. One day, I heard a knock at the door. I opened it and couldn't believe who was standing there. My life changed as soon as I looked in his eyes—it was MY DAD. He came and said we were going to move up north to Omaha, Nebraska. At that time, I didn't know what to do because I thought we were going to stay in Texas for the rest of my life. As soon as we settled down in the Midwest, we were living the same life as we had in Houston, but with a father figure.

I went to three different elementary schools because we moved from spot to spot. It was rough meeting new friends, but that's how life was. I had different friends every time we moved, but I will always remember them. Time went by and before I knew it, I was in seventh grade. My attitude wasn't straight. I was disrespectful, lazy, unprepared and didn't care what people said. I was doing bad things and getting brought home by the cops. I had no clue what I was getting into. My parents weren't expecting that from me.

For some reason, there was one person that changed my life and didn't care about how things were going. It was my middle school basketball coach, Donnie Morrison. He told me to try out for the team, and he didn't care if I was bad or not. That was the first time I played ball. I can say he changed my whole life that day. Days went by and I started liking the sport, and I wanted to get better. I listened to what he had to say. I went to practice every day. I went to the gym to work on my own. I watched basketball videos and learned new moves.

When games began, I was a starter. Everybody looked up to me. I was the hardest worker on my team. The coach loved me. My teammates gave me the ball, and to me, that meant they trusted me and they knew that I would score. It felt good to score because you get a feeling like, "Man, I'm the best, and they cannot stop me."

Now when I score, it still feels good because the crowd is making a lot of noise, and everybody is just excited. The game of basketball is really fun, regardless of if you know how to play or not. I always want to be a winner, I will always play hard, and I will never give up. When I started playing basketball, my attitude started to change. I was getting older, and I was tired of the old me. Now I am funny, outgoing, and fun to hang with. I listen to what people say. I'm respectful and have more friends. People watch my games, and I love to compete. I love basketball because it keeps me out of trouble, and it will be the only thing to get me into college. Plus, I'm really good at it.

I am finishing homework, getting tutors, going to school everyday, and taking the ACT. All of these things will get me to college, which will help me make more money, also. I plan to play professional basketball after college. College coaches are looking at me because they like what they see out of me. When I make it to the pros, that's when I'll know my life is completed because that's what I've been dreaming about.

I will always work hard and be humble to achieve my dreams. They will come true, even if it takes seven years. People are afraid to have a big dreams because they're not confident about what they will become or what they have to go through. It takes a lot of steps to get where you want to go.

In the future, I will have the money to give back to my community, to the people that helped me out in life and will give some to my country, also. One day, there will be a street that will be named after me. I will create a park for the children and even a school. Soon, everybody will be living wealthy because of what I will become.

I also look forward to being married and having children. We will be living somewhere down in the southern part of the States or live on the west coast. I have this imagined already, and I hope everything goes as well as I planned. There will be distractions, but that won't stop me from who I will become. I have big dreams to fill, but it will start by taking small steps. Success doesn't build up in one day. It takes a lot of work. Everyday, I work hard toward my goals of going to college and playing basketball, and this gives me hope for the future. Basketball is my ticket to HOPE.

"I even used my teamwork ability in the class, and it helped me excel."

Support + Opportunity = Success

Success is the end result of a simple, yet difficult mathematical equation: SUPPORT + OPPORTUNITY = SUCCESS. The support of my parents and family has given me the opportunity to play soccer, which in turn has been the greatest influence on my life, not only on the field, but also in my daily life.

The support from my family and friends has always been a tremendous help for me. They have always pushed me to do better in everything that I do, whether it be school or one of my passions. Every time I ever felt like giving up, they were there to tell me not to, to make sure I always finished what I started. They taught me that as hard as it may have seemed, nothing is impossible. They have also told me countless times that any success worth having is worth fighting for.

My family and friends have not been the only ones to help me achieve my success. My passion has also taught me. My passion is soccer. Fortunately, I have been able to play soccer at such a high, competitive level. Not only has this helped me improve in my skill as a player, but it has also helped me evolve as a person by allowing me to sharpen up some very essential life skills, one of which is teamwork.

A great example of this is the time my team went down to Minnesota and took part in Schwan's USA Cup, which is one of the top international tournaments in the country. Throughout the tournament, we weren't playing as a team. Our coach was upset with us because of how bad we were playing. It got to the point where halfway into the tourney we were about to pack our stuff to leave and go back home. That is where we reached a turning point as a team: either we fix our problem and play how we trained to play, as a team, or we forfeit the tourney and lose our chance to take part in it again. So we went back to the field knowing that we were about to face the top team of the tournament. Even though we knew how big of a challenge this would be, we went forward with it.

The game starts! They have the ball first, and they begin to move the ball around pretty well. But they had no true attack. Then, on a poorly played ball from one of their midfielders, we took it from them and had a great counterattack opportunity. It was a great shot past the keeper, but it was blocked by their post. When this happened, the other team was surprised. They began to move the ball away quickly, getting up the field. They took a great shot and scored. Our reaction to that goal was completely different than the ones we had earlier in the tourney. Instead of pointing fingers and blaming each other, we all remained calm and talked about what we needed to fix. On our kickoff, we played the ball well and quickly went up the field to score the equalizer right as the halftime whistle was about to blow. Both teams went off the field, exhausted. The remaining half of the game was very intense. There were top-quality shots and saves from both teams. We were level 'til about seven minutes left, when there was a very controversial handball in our penalty kick area. They teed the ball off and took a shot, but it was saved by our keeper. Everybody rushed in to try to get the ball away from the area. Amongst the chaos, the ball hit, deflected off one of our players and rolled in. Even though we lost that game, what we got out of it was far more important than the three points. We learned know how much teamwork is needed—not only on the field, but in life as well.

Now, as a 17-year-old senior in high school, I'm being pounded constantly with questions about college and scholarships: "Where do you want to go?" and "What do you want to study?" and "Have you applied for scholarships?" Thanks to all the support that I have received from my teachers, parents, and even soccer, I can face these questions head-on and not be completely terrified. With their support, I have been encouraged to do a lot of things which have better prepared me. This past summer, I participated in the University of Nebraska - Omaha Summer Scholars Program, which gave me the chance to take a summer class on campus and experience the college life on and off campus. It also gave me a better feel for the school and more or less how classes are run. I even used my teamwork ability in the class, and it helped me excel. Because it was a sophomore-level class, I discovered I was able to work with students I had never seen before. My teamwork experience made it a lot easier. The Summer Scholars Program was just a stepping stone for what I hope to accomplish with my post high school education. After high school, I would like to attend UNO and begin my journey to receiving first my bachelor's degree in Information Technology (IT) and my master's degree shortly afterward. I know I will still need to go back occasionally to stay up-to-date, whether it will be learning new computer terminology or more complex hardware and/or software maintenance. Staying up-to-date is important to my success, but I also hope to be actively involved in my community.

My goal is to start some small computer program work-shops in community centers, such as the Boys and Girls Club, Kroc Center and YMCA. I know many kids do not have the same opportunities that I have been given and may be involved doing wrong things with the wrong people. By delivering these workshops, I hope to give other kids the OPPORTUNITY and SUPPORT they need to complete that same simple, yet difficult, mathematical equation. When I accomplish this, I will consider my life an honest SUCCESS.

Transformations & Wisdom

"I cannot wait to accomplish my dreams. I have grown to love not only myself but others as well."

It Took Almost Losing It for Me to Appreciate It

"What are you, stupid? Why would you do this to yourself?!" My dad yelled at me while all I could think of was the pain. All the emotional pain I had bottled up inside me. Sour, nasty tears blurred my eyesight. In my head, I could see the flashback of my hands trembling, trying to open the pill bottle and then stuffing handful after handful in my mouth. I couldn't believe all that was happening, but most of all, I couldn't believe I had done this to myself. Hearing my dad's rough voice only made me feel disgusted and ashamed, as if I had committed a sin for trying to take away my life. I still had the gross aftertaste of the pills in my mouth, and I could feel the stupid IV pierce through my cold hand into my vein. I fell asleep wondering and questioning God: Why, if I was His princess, did I feel so alone and afraid?

Not knowing it was going to be an answer from God, I woke up to the annoying beep of a hospital machine next door to me, and in the far distance, the soft voices of whispering nurses and doctors. I got out of bed looking for my mom. As I stepped out of my room, I looked to the room next door to me where the beeping noise was coming from. Inside the room, I saw a little boy sound asleep. The TV was on mute, but the Backyardigans was on. I stared at the little boy, and I wondered why he was there. Why weren't his parents there with him? I don't know how long I stared at him, but I do know it was for a while because when the nurse walked into the room she made me jump. I asked the nurse why he had yellow skin and why he was there. She explained to me that he had been here for a few months because he was waiting for a liver transplant, and his parents were unable to be with him. She told me that this little boy and his family were from a different city, and they were home working to pay the hospital bill. I walked back to my room in silence with a knot in my throat. I couldn't believe I had purposely damaged my liver, and this cute little boy didn't have an option and unlike me he was completely alone. He needed what I had taken for granted.

On many occasions, I felt as if I was the only one walking around with a problem. I felt alone and disoriented, not noticing all the people that were trying to help me. On those chilly December mornings, I hardly ever wanted to get out of bed. I wanted to stay under my covers and pretend school didn't exist because homework only seemed to pile up. But staying at home wasn't an option; teachers and my family weren't going to let me give up on myself like that. One teacher in particular was kind, sweet, and understanding to me. When I sat in front of her, she talked not like a teacher to student, but like someone that cared about me. She explained to me that I didn't need a man to be happy. That I need to love and be happy with myself first, and whenever I would find the perfect person he would only add to my happiness. Even though I felt lonesome, I knew I had my wonderful family that I could trust with my problems.

One morning, I woke up to my sister's high-pitched voice, telling me it was time for school. I hardly wanted to get out of bed but I did—only because she was physically pulling me out of bed. I arrived at school late like many times before. When I got out of my car, it was a frosty, snowy morning, and I could see my breath in the air. I thought to myself, "Why did I even come?" As I walked into my classroom twenty minutes after the late bell, all eyes were on me, even the teacher's. I knew exactly what ran through their minds: "She's sooo lazy. Isn't she embarrassed for being late ALL the time?" I sat down in my seat full of embarrassment. I hated being late, and most of all I hated the thoughts that ran through people's minds. I wasn't what they thought. I wasn't lazy, and I didn't want people to think that. My days at school felt like eternity. I dreaded being at school not because I disliked school but because I felt discouraged and uncomfortable. At night, I prayed, and I hoped that God would give me strength and courage to get up the next morning.

I believe that God gave us parents accordingly in our lives so that they could guide us and help us through our troubles. And like many times before, my mother was always there to comfort me with her gentle words and her warm hugs. On one particular night after my hospital stay, I was in my room, and everything felt so distant, cold and quiet. I hated this feeling only because it made me feel alone—not only emotionally, but physically. This great sadness filled me, and again, bad thoughts popped into my head. Maybe it was a mother's instinct, but my mom rushed into my room, and she hugged me so tightly and warmly that I could smell the food she was cooking. This reminded me of when I was a little girl and I would watch as she made fresh homemade tortillas. As she rolled out each tortilla, my mouth would water, and I wanted her to be done so badly so I could have one. She would put a little pinch of salt on the tortilla and roll it up into a taco for me and my sister to eat. Almost instantly, I felt as if things were going to get better because she gave me something that I needed—hope.

Hope for me means to have faith in something that can be obtained through God's help. Throughout my difficulty, I let others help me. I never lost faith, but most of all, I had hope. At first, the purpose of my problem was unseen, but as months went by, I realized it was for me to appreciate my life, my surroundings, and the people that love me. Now it's nearly six months until I graduate, and it seems like yesterday that graduation felt almost impossible. My experience has brought hope into the future, and I cannot wait to accomplish my dreams. I have grown to love not only myself but others as well. Staring at the "little boy" now makes more sense to me now than it did before; I want to be there for those who really don't have an option. I still wonder what happened to that little boy, but it brings great satisfaction knowing that I will be there to help other kids like him. Next year, I plan to enroll at a college and become a nurse for chronic illnesses. After college, I hope to have an amazing family and be the kind of mother and wonderful wife that other great women have shown me how to be.

"You can't change the past,
but you can always
change the future."

Unbreakable

Even though I walk through the valley of the shadow of death, I will fear no evil for you are with me.
- Psalm 23:4

I've done some things that I would have never imagined that I would do.

It all started with the first hit and then I was hooked. The first time I experienced marijuana, I was 14. I was with a group of guys, drinking, then all of a sudden they started rolling a blunt of marijuana. I was hoping they wouldn't ask me to take a hit because I'd never tried anything like that before. Unfortunately, they did, and I finally gave in because I was curious. As I took the first hit, I felt very strange, but then after a few more hits, I felt happy. Around that time, I wasn't feeling very happy about my life and I started liking this drug that kept a smile on my face. It made me laugh and feel lost in my little world. Little did I know that getting lost in my own little world would be a bad thing for me.

When I was younger, I always felt like I never belonged, so many people would take advantage of me because I was so nice. People would walk all over me simply because they didn't care. I always wanted my father in my life so we could have that father-and-daughter bond that so many children have with their fathers. My dad died when I was 2 years old, and even if I never knew him, I know he loved me with all his heart. I always wanted him in my life when I needed him the most to tell me how amazing he thinks I am and that he thinks I'm beautiful even if no one else thought I was. I never felt beautiful or important to anyone. I always felt like a joke to everyone, and I felt that no one took me seriously. I would often look up to the stars and tell

51

my daddy to make all the pain go away. I never thought any guy would be able to like me, but when a guy finally did, I fell head over heels for him. I wish my daddy could've been here so he could've warned me that guys would want to use me and then leave me, but I didn't, and I was left heartbroken and feeling worthless.

I really didn't smoke much in the beginning, but after my ex-boyfriend and I broke up, I felt very sad and depressed. I felt useless and alone and like the one thing that could make me happy was marijuana. The more I smoked, the more I started depending on this drug; I would go to school high and sometimes even smoke inside school. I started skipping classes my freshmen year, but the year that I really started skipping and smoking a lot more was my sophomore year. It started getting bad when I smoked weed in the girl's restroom with my friend and someone smelled the strong scent of marijuana coming from the restroom. We managed to get out in time before the teachers got there, but the security camera saw us come out of the school bathroom, and they called us both down to the administrator's office, and they found drug paraphernalia in my backpack. I got suspended for 19 days, and the school made me take some classes about drug abuse. I also had to do some AA classes in order to go back to school. The worst part of getting caught in school was that I got a letter from court telling me that I had a charge because of the drug paraphernalia that I had in my backpack. I ended up getting probation, which would've been okay if I really was doing what I was supposed to do, but I was so into the lifestyle of smoking weed that I simply didn't care. I would still continue to skip school and smoke on a daily basis. I failed more than six drug tests when they all came out positive for marijuana. Finally, my probation officer told me that if I didn't calm down and start doing what I was supposed to do, the judge was going to lock me up. I started passing my drug tests and I stopped skipping. The judge then decided that she saw me improve, and after seven months of being in probation she finally let me out of the system. When I got out of the system, I still wasn't determined to stop. I felt I had no reason to stop. The first thing I did the same day I got out of the system was buy some marijuana and get lost in the clouds, like before. Once I started smoking again, it started just going downhill from the moment that I took a hit.

By the time I hit my junior year, I started skipping classes. Since I was failing all my classes, I gave up on myself completely. I felt useless when I would go to class. I felt like I was just taking up a seat that someone else deserved. Skipping three periods a day turned into skipping every single day 'til I finally stopped showing up. Everyone that I trusted turned their back on me when I needed them the most. They started talking behind my back, saying I was worthless and that I would never change. It only made me feel more down and made me want to smoke more. I felt no one understood me because they never took the time to listen to me. Everyone just judged me. I lost a lot of friends because of this habit, but nothing compared to the respect and the trust I lost from my family. I felt that I was a mistake and that I didn't belong in this world for putting my mom through hell. Just seeing her beautiful eyes cry killed me inside.

The more I tried to stop smoking, the more it felt like the marijuana wouldn't let me. Sometimes when there wasn't marijuana to smoke, I would do other drugs, and I've tried the craziest drugs out there. I would pray to God at night and ask him to help me out because I was determined to stop smoking and change for my mom. But in order to change for her, I had to do it for myself first. Then, junior year ended, and it got me very upset to know that in the past three years of school, I only had sophomore credits. No words in this world can explain how much it hurt to finally realize that I was probably not going to graduate on time. When I realized how this situation was going to affect me in the future, I was determined to stop. When I was giving up completely, something in my heart told me that I can do it, and I know it was God telling me this. I knew that it wasn't going to be easy trying to change, but just knowing that God was right beside me gave me the hope that I needed. My Lord is my strength, my best friend, my everything. He's the only one I can truly say never, ever gave up on me. He was always there with me, holding my hand, guiding the way.

When I was smoking, I realized that the marijuana was hurting me in a physical way. It was making me gain weight. I would eat all the time, even when I wasn't hungry. I also stopped caring about my appearance. I figured that no one even liked me anyway, so I saw no point in trying. I also started noticing that as I looked at my reflection in the mirror, I wasn't happy with the girl that I was becoming. My self-esteem was so low that I felt clueless and depressed all the time. When I would get high, I was happy, but as soon as my high started going down again, I would be sad and feel alone inside. I felt that the marijuana was hurting me not only in a physical way but also in an emotional way. My mind wasn't thinking clearly; I felt like it was in some other planet. I knew that I was taking it too far when I spend so much money on weed. I tried to stop buying weed, but eventually I would end up buying more. As I look back, I feel very sad to know that all those hours at work didn't pay off at all because I would spend it all a couple days after I would get my check.

The number one reason that I wanted to stop smoking was for my mother, the most amazing lady to walk this earth. Growing up as a single mother at the age of 26 and having to raise three little girls after my dad died when I was barely a little girl must have been very hard for her, but my mother never lost hope, even if hope was the only choice she had. My mother came from Mexico to America to give me and my sisters a better life and more opportunities than what we had in Mexico. My mother has taught me the amazing strength and love that a mother has for her children. No words in this entire world can describe the love I have for this beautiful lady. She has impacted my life in so many ways. She has taught me everything I know in life. Without her, I wouldn't know what to do; she's my blessing from the heavens above. Most importantly, when the world gave up on me, my mother always had hope that someday, I would change. I look up to my mother because someday I want to be as strong as her.

I cannot wait for the day that I get my diploma. I know that it is going to be the happiest day in my life; just knowing that I've made this day become possible will be an amazing feeling. The reason I will be even happier is to know that I made my mom proud of me. To see a big smile in her beautiful face will fill me with joy. So many people have doubted me all my life, saying that I wasn't good enough, but I want to prove them all wrong the day that I get my diploma. My dream has always been to go to college, and I don't care what I have to do to accomplish this dream. I will make that happen. As I look at my life in the future, I see myself having an amazing career that I enjoy, which would probably be a detective, counselor, or a librarian. It probably won't really matter which one I choose because all three of these jobs involve working with people. I see myself becoming a mature young lady in society and becoming more independent than I already am. The day that I have children of my own, I want them to be proud of their mom and to be able to look up to me instead of looking down on me. I want them to know that I'm willing to do whatever in the world I have to do for them. I want to be a Latina who accomplishes a lot in life, not another statistic of what the world thinks of us. The day I die, I want to be remembered as someone who never gave up and was willing to follow her heart. I want to be remembered for the great things that I accomplish, not the negative things that I have done.

Looking back at the dumb mistakes that I made in the past makes me want to look forward and not dwell on the past. You can't change the past, but you can always change the future. Making mistakes is normal. It helps you to learn right from wrong and to make you understand and open up your eyes. Just take it from a person who has been through some mistakes in life. Just remember to always stay positive and to always believe in yourself. Even when it seems that the world gave up on you, it doesn't mean that you have to do the same things as everyone else. Before you start getting tempted to smoke weed, think about it really clearly. You might feel that it's cool at the moment to smoke to fit in, but the only one that you're hurting is yourself. If I could open up everyone's eyes about doing drugs, I would. It's not that it's bad for you, but it messes up your life. If I could take back everything I've done, I would, but I know that's not possible. What I did in my past made me who I am today. It made me a stronger person, and for the first time in my life, I feel *unbreakable*.

*"Court was no joke.
I never went to a courtroom
in my life, and I was
so nervous."*

A New Outlook on Life

No matter what you go through or what you have done, you can do anything if you have hope. It's like "Pandora's Box." She opened a box that Zeus gave her, and then all the bad and evil things came out and plagues spread like wildfire. All that was left was hope. I'm not saying my situation is as bad as Pandora's, but it's not a good one, either. I didn't really have hope at first … only after reality hit me in the face, and I got in some serious trouble with the law. That is when I started to hope it would all go away, but it didn't. Here's my story …

I wasn't a bad student at all. My sister and I were always tardy or absent from school, even in elementary. So we went to a program to help me so I would not be late anymore, but we moved and I stopped attending the program. I continued to be late. I don't even know why I was late. I just wanted to follow in my older sister's footsteps. And I did exactly that. When I got to high school, I started to skip every morning because I didn't like my first hour teacher. By not going to class and not getting my credits, I was only hurting myself. Being late became a bad habit of mine, though I didn't think anything of it at the time. "I was late, and what are they going to do about it? Nothing …" Well, I was wrong.

It was now my sophomore year, and my mother was opening her mail. My sister and I got a court date for truancy. Court was no joke. I never went to a courtroom in my life, and I was so nervous. We had to pass through a metal detector, and it started to go off when I walked past it and my mom stared at me with this evil eye. You know—when your parents are mad at you, they give you that look and you just *know*. Now I'm extremely nervous, but I found out it went off because of my lip ring. I felt so relieved. We got to the elevator and pressed the button for sixth floor, the top floor. When I got there, there were bars over the ledge and I asked my mom why it was there. She replied that it was so kids wouldn't jump over the ledge. I was in shock. Who would want to do that? We checked in and took our seats, then waited for our names to be called. Finally, we heard the bailiff call us. She led us to our seats. I felt like I was on one of those court shows on TV. We had to stand up when the judge walked in and only sat when he said we could sit – but there was no audience. Before it even started, the judge read us our rights really fast. I didn't understand much of that, all I could remember him saying was "You have a right to a speedy trial." It was over before I knew it. We were court-ordered to have a probation officer, counseling, and to go to a truancy program.

My probation officer had no confidence in us at all. We saw her at least once a week. My mother said she looked like a crack head, which in my eyes, too, she kind of did. The weirdest thing I had to do was the pee test to see if I have taken any drugs … which I haven't because I'm such an angel, right?

Counseling was a different story. We saw our therapist every Thursday, and we were dismissed from her early. My probation officer wasn't too pleased about that.

The truancy program was nice, I guess. It was at Boys and Girls Club, and over there it was called the Noble Youth Group. I met a very influential person named Beto Gonzalez. He was short-statured and had a Spanish accent. When he said "education" he would say it like "edge-a-ma-cation." He made things interesting so we would understand things, and he told us why we shouldn't skip school, do drugs, and other bad things. I didn't really talk in the group because most of the people had it really bad. My situation is not as bad as theirs. He could relate to everyone. Beto also came out of a bad childhood, but he had faith and hope, and he got out of the bad situation and got far in life. I was determined to follow his example. It was rocky at first. I was late a couple of times, and I improved slowly and progressed bit by bit. Now I am not late at all anymore, so they closed out my case and I was free. Well, not really, but I felt so relieved! I still have to live under my mom's rules, but no more pee tests and weekly visits with my probation officer.

I found out how fun school can be—all the clubs, after-school activities, and the Band room. I got kicked out of Concert Band my freshman year because of the truancy issue. Since then, I got my act together and joined Band again, then reacquainted with my old friends that were in there. I would skip lunch and go to the Band room so we could go on Garage Band. Garage Band is when you make music on the computer.

My friends made a rap crew, which was made of Daniel, Jasmine, and Alyssa. I like to watch them. I'm not that good with rapping, but I made a few. I thought Daniel made the funniest raps. So when I started to go to Band again I met Jasmine, who suggested that I should go to Gay Straight Alliance (GSA), and that's what I did. It was fun, and we talked about deep things like how offensive it is when people say "That's gay" or call us "fag-got." Every Monday, Wednesday, and Friday I would stay after school for JROTC. There are new people in JROTC every year, so I make even more friends each year. My friends are my main reason why I come to school. They are my motivation. If I didn't have them, I would probably have dropped out of school a long time ago.

So now I'm taking summer school and taking Saturday classes so I can earn my credits that I didn't get on time and try to graduate in December. Me go to college? A year ago I would have said no, but now I have a different perspective on life. I want to earn a degree in accounting so I can help my mom out and take care of her in the future. My mom took care of me when I was little. When my friends came over, they thought she was mad all the time. Though my mother's tone of voice made her sound angry, I could always tell when my mom was joking around. I always appreciated her sense of humor.

Now it's my turn to take care of her. Those are my family values. I'll figure out the money issue for college later. I have time until then. That just goes to show you: If you have hope, you can do anything with your life.

"Teenagers think it's so easy, that life's always going to be there, but they don't see that bad things can always happen, that life can be gone in the blink of an eye."

Life on the Tilt

When you think of friends, you think that they'll always be there to support you through the rough times. Then when something actually bad happens, you realize the only people who will always be there are your family. My family learned this the hard way. It's my hope that others realize the importance of family before it's too late.

As I grew up I always had both my parents there to support me and love me. I was like four years old when my baby sister was born. We lived in these ghetto apartments with lots of *cucarachas* and flies roaming around. I don't remember my parents fighting too often unless my dad and his friends were drinking. They didn't know their limit. My dad and his friends would hang out and drink outside our house. My mom told me that she kicked my dad's friends out of the house, and he got mad. My dad—I love him so much—he is a great guy—always treated us like his queens; my sister, my mom, and me. But when he was drunk, all the love seemed to fade away. He was a different guy with a really bad temper, and he would sometimes scare me just by the way he would act.

Alcoholism: dependence on alcohol consumption to an extent that adversely affects social and work-related functioning and produces withdrawal symptoms when intake is stopped or greatly reduced.

As the years went along, not much changed, my dad would still drink, and mom wouldn't like it. One night my dad was drinking with his friends, and I don't recall what ticked off him off, but he started going crazy! He was yelling, and then next thing I knew, there was blood dripping down his arm. He was so mad that he punched the living room window, breaking it with his fist and cutting himself. I remember crying, and I was confused. My mom just wanted to get us out of the house and away from my dad. That's when we left with our family friends, and my dad just ran down the street chasing after us. We drove back to the house because my mom had forgotten something and when we arrived I saw the ambulance. They took my dad to the hospital even though he didn't want to go. He said he was fine, but there was still blood dripping down his arm. He ended up running away from the hospital! We were worried because he wasn't being himself, so we wondered where he would go. Luckily, he was fine. Weeks passed, and then something happened that would change him and our family for the better.

He woke up on the side of the freeway passed out. Again, my dad had got lucky and nothing happened. But eventually, he got arrested and put in jail. All this had happened in such little time, a few weeks before, my dad had gotten arrested for drunk driving. I had gone with him to one of his court hearings, and that's when they announced to him he had to do about a month of nights in jail and to attend AA meetings. One night, my mom and dad were talking about who would be picking him up at 4 a.m. from jail. My dad struggled to find a friend to do him that favor, and this is where he learned his lesson. His friends were just around for the times that he had booze, but when he actually needed someone's help, they had disappeared. I remember waking up to my parents hugging each other before he had to leave to go to jail. Although he wasn't going to be there for long, it was hard because he wouldn't be around much. Every weekday, my mom woke us up at 3:30 a.m. to go get my dad and then we would come back home to sleep for a bit before he headed off to work and us to school. When my dad was out, we were happy as could be, and from this point on, things started to change.

We spent more time as a family, and he wouldn't waste his work checks on an illness that could've taken his life away. Of course, in the beginning, it was hard for my dad to quit so drastically, but with his family by his side we did it. There's been so many times that my dad's told me, *Tus estudios son los que te van a sacar adelante, tus amigos no.* Now it's been seven years since my dad's been sober, and we're so thankful that our life changed because not everyone's family can achieve what we did. Sadly, some families split up or they even might lose a loved one because of this illness!

It was our first trip to Mexico, and we were all happy and excited to meet the rest of our family for the first time. I think my mom was the one who was the most excited because she was finally going to be able to see her parents, who she hadn't seen in 12 years. When we arrived *a la terminal,* it was late at night, and we waited anxiously for my *Tío May* to pick us up. As we got closer to my grandparents' house, I felt butterflies in my stomach. The next thing we saw was a bunch of my cousins and *tíos* running out of my grandparent's house rushing toward us, everyone hugging us and tears rolling down their cheeks. Days passed, and one day we were outside getting ready to eat and some old-looking guy walked in trying to sell some sculptures of the Virgin Mary and of various cartoon characters. He looked so beat up and very dirty, with clothes that seemed to be what he wore every day. Once he started talking to my mom, I realized she knew him from her childhood, and his name was Alfredo. I remember my mom telling him that she wasn't going to buy anything from him if he was going to use the money to buy alcohol, but he said he wouldn't. The next day he walked to the back yard again, and he sent one of my cousins to go get him a bottle of rubbing alcohol and a pop. I was like *Okay…?* Then, when my cousin got back, he mixed the rubbing alcohol with the pop! I was surprised; he was drinking it as if it was normal beer or something. The *rancho* where my mom is from isn't that big, so I would see him every day wandering around drunk. A couple of weeks passed. It was around Christmas time when one afternoon he picked up my baby brother, Daniel. This memory has stayed with me. At the time Daniel was one year old. Alfredo picked him up and stared at him for the longest time. Then he said, "*Este niño va ser que yo cambie*" meaning "this child is going to make me change." After we left Mexico, mom told me that Alfredo had changed; that he had moved in with an uncle of his out of the *rancho* and that he was working and staying sober. Eventually, he moved back and he fell into his old ways again. I remember asking my mom why he was always alone, and if he had a family, and she told me he did. She told me that he was married to one of my cousin's relatives and that he had two kids: a girl and a boy. He was no longer with them due to his drinking. He had lost is family, his home and his kids. I went back to Mexico in the summer of '09, and I saw him again. He looked older, more beat up, and as usual he was still an alcoholic. He hung out with younger guys who drank also, and I hoped they wouldn't follow his footsteps. After my visit that year, I haven't gone back but my mom told me that he had passed away. He died because his drinking was so bad, he was drinking rubbing alcohol, and that destroyed his liver. By then, it was too late for him. He didn't have the chance my dad had to fix things with his family because he hadn't learned from his mistakes. The saddest part is that he was a husband and a father, but he lost everything. Now I hope he's in a better place.

My summer of '09 was amazing! I was in Mexico with my family, and we had just arrived there a couple of days before. Like usual when we're there, the *pachanga* had to get started. I was at my dad's mom's house, and they had a *comida* for my little cousins that had just got out of elementary school. Where we're from, the end of school means "let's have a get-together!" So we were there enjoying the time together. My *Tía* Male—she is the tightest *tía* I could have—she knows how to have a blast, so there we were, taking shots of tequila, and I was pretty stable until the night came. I was at a quince with my *prima* Suzy and her friend and another friend named Adán, and we were all drinking, and oh man! I started feeling messed up! During the party, I could barely keep myself up anymore, so I was just holding onto Adán. I was so wasted by then, my cousin Suzy and Adán took me home. When I was going to get ready to fall asleep I start feeling nauseous, and next thing I knew, I start throwing up into a trashcan and my *Tía* Male was holding my hair back. I was so drunk that I was calling for my mom, but my mom was nowhere near because she had stayed in Omaha. After a while, I was knocked out on the toilet seat, and from that point on I don't remember anything.

The next morning, I had such a huge hangover, and to make things worse, I had to wake up super early because my dad's family wanted to go up to the mountains and just have a fun day, which for me wasn't so fun! Oh my gosh, afterwards I could not stand the smell of tequila or the sun because I would immediately throw up. It lasted the whole day up till the nighttime, and I sure learned about crossing drinks! Hangovers are not for me, and they can sometimes just cause you embarrassing moments.

Both my dad and I learned our lessons. He wasn't so happy when I told him about my summer incident because he immediately told me that he didn't want us falling onto the same path he did. Teenagers think it's so easy, that life's always going to be there, but they don't see that bad things can always happen, that life can be gone in the blink of an eye. I hope that by after reading my story, people (not only teenagers, but everyone) take the opportunity to make the right choices and learn from other people's mistakes. Trying to feel "cool" and drink every weekend can seem like a fun thing now, but they might not realize that they can be leading themselves to a lifetime full of disasters.

"I think the only answer is to start believing in myself and realizing that I can accomplish great things."

It's Never Too Late

The other day in class, I got asked the infamous question: "Where do you want to be in ten years?" As I was thinking to myself, I thought, "I don't even know where I'm going to be in 10 minutes!" But then I really thought about it—where *do* I want to be in ten years? I thought of all the things I could hope for, and all the things I ever wanted to do to make my future and the future a bright one.

For myself, I could only hope that I'm going to be happy with whatever I'm doing in ten years. As much as I hope these good things happen to me, it's up to ME to decide the outcome of MY future. After high school, there's no more depending on people to clean up my messes. But if I do end up being wealthy, not just in money but in mind and spirit as well, what kind of person would I be to not credit the ones who have helped me and shaped me?

Throughout my lifetime, in my eyes I haven't done much to be proud of. My grades have always been average or below average. I remember sitting at the kitchen table with my mom when I was younger, crying my eyes out about doing my homework. Looking back, I don't remember if it was the fact that I didn't understand it, or just simply because I didn't want to do it. Nowadays, I realize I didn't do it because I didn't understand it. I didn't understand it because I didn't pay attention in class.

I've come to understand that the partying, disrespecting and lying to my parents, skipping class and blowing off homework was probably the last thing I should have been doing. I started smoking cigarettes when I was in eighth grade, and eventually I started smoking weed almost every day. It was my escape. All the growing up I tried to do then, by doing what at the time what I thought was cool and being adult-like, I'm making up for now.

73

I'm seventeen years old, never had a job, and still haven't even gotten my learner's permit.

How should I expect to be moving out, going to school, and working after I graduate? Right now, it seems impossible, and it's scary to me. Soon, I think I'm not going to be able to rely on anybody but myself. I have to start getting my priorities straight. Not only for me, but so that my family—particularly my father—can see me grow into a successful, independent young woman.

I recently found out that my father has a disease called pulmonary fibrosis. After months of testing, and a lung biopsy later, he was diagnosed. It literally broke my heart to see him hooked up to an oxygen machine and lying in a hospital bed. He tells my sister and I not to worry about him, but it's so hard not to. My father is a very strong man. He has the support of his family and friends all around him, so he will never be alone in his struggle. My parents got a divorce when I was eleven. Since then, me and my dad have not been as close as we could be. This disease coming upon him has made me open my eyes to realize what is really important, and that's building our relationship and making him proud of me.

After my parents got a divorce, my mother's stress came to a level I have never seen before. Stress about finances, about me and my schoolwork, about her and her work. The stress had a huge effect on me because my mother does not handle her stress well. She would drink a lot, and we would get in arguments that would turn physical. I never thought it was right, her hitting me, but I'm sure I deserved it. As I got older and more mature, the fighting died down a lot. But regardless of it being gone now, it was there once. I can't blame my mom; I wasn't being the easiest teenager to deal with, never listening and always doing the opposite of what I was told.

When I look back at all the stupid choices I have made that have disappointed my parents, the thing I regret most is not being closer to my dad and listening—*really* listening—to what him and my mother had to say. I think if I would have been closer to my dad and listened to him, I wouldn't be in the state of panic I'm in now with graduation around the corner.

Sometimes I feel like I have to amount to something so great that's it's never going to happen because I'm not capable of it. It's almost like people expected more out of me than I have to give. Thinking about this standard I have to live up to but that hasn't necessarily been set for me really gets me down. It is depressing when people are constantly expecting the worst from you. But I have also heard that if I don't have faith in myself, how can I expect anybody else to? I have not quite found the answer to that question. I think the only answer is to start believing in myself and realizing I can accomplish great things.

So what it comes down to is me believing in myself and knowing that if I work hard, all the things in my past will not matter. It's about my future now. It always has been, and it just took me a while to realize it. Even with a shady past, it is never too late. It is never too late to turn it around and be something great. With the motivation I have around me, in ten years, I'm going to be just fine.

"I had empathy even though
I did not know them.
Seeing the way they lived
their lives is what
changed me."

Determination and the Three Cs

Three years ago, I walked though the prison, and that is when my life changed. At the time, I was careless and I hung out with the wrong people, which led me into trouble. That day, I decided I would focus on my future and make better decisions. I felt that there was something better for me down the road, and I was determined to make a change.

I have overcome many obstacles in my life, and I have learned a lot the hard way. I learned that you have to take chances and never back down. Being negative will get you nowhere. Believe in yourself to make dreams come true. Nothing is given to you. I have worked hard for what I want and did not give up. I hope to make a difference. I may be young, but I have big ideas. My experiences have made me who I am today and made me think a lot about how I want my future to be. Everyone makes mistakes; it's not wrong, it's life. Through determination, I have learned, and that is how I got my life back on track.

When I walked into the prison, I was not the same person as when I came out. Before that day, I was almost taken away from my mom. I was being a follower instead of a leader. I did not have set goals, either. I didn't even stop to think about college. I just thought about partying and hanging with friends. It wasn't until 2007 when that all changed. I had to take a tour of the prison for my probation class, and it was not a pretty sight. It was like living a day in the shoes of an inmate. I had empathy even though I did not know them. Seeing the way they lived their lives is what changed me. I couldn't imagine myself living that way for the rest of my life and not being able to see my loved ones. It would feel like you were a bird in a cage.

Your freedom is completely taken away once you are inside. There would be no privacy, especially if you were sharing a cell.

When you have to shower, people watch. Even to go to the bathroom—the toilet is in your cell and in most cells, it is at the end of the bed. Can you imagine sleeping and smelling your roommate's feces all night? It's like being trapped on an island all alone, and no one is there to save you. You would feel isolated. It would be cold, and there would be no color, just black and gray. In prison, the only color there would be is the neon orange of the jumpsuits that everyone is required to wear. Walking through the halls, you hear people fighting or arguing. It's not peaceful at all. On every floor, there is a guard who is kind of like a watch-dog. On every cell door, there is a number, and that number is your home. It is like your address. It represents you. I imagine the Holocaust and how all the people had their names taken away. They had numbers tattooed on their wrists to represent them. It was like their identity was erased.

Two inmates that day had to talk to us. It was like a lecture about why to change our life because they regret what they did and there's no going back for them. They told us this was our chance to change. I remember I was the only girl there that day. There was this "gangster boy" who thought it was all a joke. He had a smirk on his face. After a prisoner told him off, the so-called "gangster" was crying. Sometimes, people don't get second chances, and that was an opportunity for me. That was my time to make a change, my second chance. After that, I got my act together. I started focusing on school and stopped hanging with the people who got me into trouble. Since then, I have been very serious about my life because I want to make something of myself.

On October 4, 2008, I met someone with the same mindset as me. He is focused, and we have a lot of the same values. It helped me a lot knowing that we have been through a lot of the same experiences. Knowing that he was there by my side and he believed in me pushed me harder. He helped me and never let me give up. He knows I have the capability to do what I want to do, and so does he. He has made me have better values and standards for what I look for in a person and a husband. He has given me a lot of hope for my future, especially for having a family and raising children. Two years ago, before I met him, I never thought I would find "The One," but because I had hope I met him. We have been through many ups and downs, and we know each other's strengths and weaknesses. He gave me a lot of hope for my future. We have become very strong and have a really strong relationship, and building trust helps. You can't let anyone bring you down or get in the way, and we have overcome a lot of obstacles together. He uses this really cute quote he got from the movie *Kung Fu Panda*: "Yesterday is history, tomorrow is a mystery, but today is a gift. That is why it's called the present." I think it is a really great quote that has a lot of meaning to it. Needless to say, having someone by your side to help and encourage you gives you more hope. One day, we hope to get married and have children.

This is my last year walking through the halls again, hearing the bells ring to go to class. I am a senior, and this is my year, the year that matters the most. I have set goals for what I want to do after I graduate. I want to go to college and get my four-year degree and I want to become a registered nurse. I hope to work in the NICU with the babies who need my help. I am taking a class to get my CNA, and I am getting a head start on my career. I love animals, and I am very passionate about helping them. When I was younger, I saw my dog abused. He almost died and still to this day, I am against animal abuse. I would like to be a vet tech or just volunteer with animals. That way, I'll know I'm helping them and making a difference in their life. Just recently, I applied to Iowa Western Community College for the vet tech program, and I was accepted. So it goes to show that you don't have to make up your mind about what you want to do right away. I know I am still not sure exactly what I want to do, but I know it will be something involving helping babies or animals. Either way, I got a head start on both of the careers I'm looking into. I know who I am as a person, and just to think, three years ago, I had no idea who I actually was or what I wanted. I took everything as a joke. I thought that school was boring and dumb. I didn't care about my grades, but it all changed in one day. School now to me is the key to my future. I am doing all I can to get to my career going. I just have to stay focused and not let anyone tell me different.

When I think about my future ten years from now, I will be married to my boyfriend and have two beautiful children named Isabella and Isaac. Family is a really important to me because since I was small, I never really had my biological dad around. My mom raised me. I had father figures to fill in his place but not my actual dad. He was never there. For my children, both me and my husband will be there in their lives. I think they'll deserve it. I don't want my kids to grow up with parents in different places, like I did. I think that has impacted my life not in a bad way, but for me personally, it made me stronger without my biological father around. I intend to set a good example for my kids so that when they grow up, they don't make the same mistakes I did. I know they're not going to be perfect, but I at least hope they will take my advice. I want to show them what is important in life. I wish for them to take it seriously, but I know everyone learns from their own mistakes.

Though my past experiences made me who I am today, I say always take advice from people older than you because they know better. They're not trying to lecture you; they are trying to help you out so you don't mess up. I know what I want to do for my future now. It's up to me to make it happen. Don't ever say you can't do something or it's too late because I used to be a juvenile delinquent and now I'm a completely different person with a whole different mindset. It took a lot of mistakes to change me and shape me into the person I am today. Don't give up; there is always hope. Without hope, I would not be where I am today. In ten years, I hope to make a change and impact somebody's life for the better. I want people to remember who I am. I want to make something of myself.

I'm not the same girl who walked into high school as a freshman, careless and just thinking high school was fun and games. I did a complete turnaround to who I am today, compared to who I was then. It was my hope that helped me change. Everyone has the will to change; it's just about wanting to *do* it. Do not let people influence you to do things you don't want to do. Be you; that is the only person you have to make proud. In the end, if you do things just to impress your friends, you are not going to be happy with the result. Follow your heart and set your mind to what you want to do, and you can do anything you want to do. I've learned there are three Cs in life: choices, chances and changes. You must make a choice to take a chance ... or your life will never change.

Persevering After Loss

"Strive for what you believe in and what you want to do in life."

Life Beyond Mom

This is the secret I've been keeping. I'm going to tell you about the side of me no one really knows. People think of me as the girl who doesn't seem to have problems and is always happy. But ever since I was about ten years old, my mother hasn't seemed the same as she used to when I was younger. She used be an everyday house wife and a caregiver to her children, just a regular mom taking her kids to school everyday and making sure we had a great day. She made dinner every night for the family and enjoyed the company of her husband and children.

Every day of my life since the change, my mother has struggled with paranoia problems. She believes that people are out to steal her identity, that people are all in a conspiracy together trying to take mom's and her children's identities, too. She thinks if we receive mail and our name is misspelled, then it's someone else trying to be us. Every day, she bickers, fights, throws tantrums and yells. It's been getting worse.

Every day, I have to listen to her say these things that we as a family don't understand, and we have fallen apart because of this. Every day, I hear her yell at my father, saying "It's all your fault," screaming at him, throwing things, saying "I'm not Vicky with an I!" and having hostile behaviors. Every day, I have to listen to her when we're in the car, muttering things under her breath that are completely crazy. It's like she has two sides of her. I feel like I lost my mom.

About a year ago, I suffered a miscarriage, which was hard. The doctor told me that it was just a natural thing, that "You know, sometimes if you plant a seed it doesn't grow." I cried and cried and wondered why it happened to me, and then I realized maybe it was for a reason. When I was pregnant, my dad made me feel like I was never going to amount to anything in life anymore, but I knew that wasn't true. Hearing that from my dad was very hard, but I knew I was going to strive for my best in the situation I was in. My mother told me after the whole thing happened that I probably just staged the whole thing and that it didn't really happen. Again, me not understanding the things my mom says. I am still currently with my boyfriend who I had the miscarriage with and hope to have him in my future, hopefully as my husband someday. He knows everything about my family and me. He always is there for me when I need him, which is great.

Our house is now full of things we don't even need. It drives me crazy just walking in the house. My dad is the only one who supports our family; my mom hasn't worked a paying job since we've been born. It's hard to support five people and pay all the bills. On top of everything else, my mother has a gambling problem and steals money from my dad to gamble. Since my mom started running up bills and using credit cards, my dad didn't really have any more money to keep his electrical repair shop open. He had to shut it down, and it was sad to see that happen because he did that all on his own.

My mother was admitted into a recovery center this past year for attempted suicide. She tried overdosing on pills, but my father found her lying alone in her father's house. He asked if she was okay, and she replied that she was. My father knew something was wrong; she started throwing up and told my dad to take her to the hospital. It was sad to know my mom would go to such extremes to not be here anymore, but all we want is for her to get help and she doesn't understand that. My mom is still the same and is not showing any progress or even trying to change.

When my mom starts to yell in the house, there is no stopping her, and it's hard to be at home. I can't even watch TV because she's right there saying things like, "Oh, they really want you. That's why they would take your picture. They're trying to steal our identity, and I know it; I'm right, you guys are just all in on it." When that happens, I usually walk down the street to hang out with friends. Most of the time, school comes into play with things I can do to get away, which led to me playing sports such as soccer, volleyball, track, swimming, basketball and wrestling. I always was an active person, so I liked playing sports, and it was a stress reliever, also. Sports taught me respect, leadership and teamwork. Nowadays, I still play sports, but I have narrowed it down to just soccer. It's my favorite sport, and since now I work, I don't have the time to play anything else.

Even though my family is dysfunctional, I still need to think of myself and not focus so much on the problems of my family, but instead the problems I need to face in the real world. I plan to go to college, but knowing my financial need, it's hard to say if I'm going to go or not. I'm working on applying for scholarships and soon will be taking the ACT. It's a little nerve-racking, but I have to stay focused. I want to attend college when I graduate from high school. My passion is to design and do hands-on creative projects. I have an eye for things; I'm also good at placing objects to make them look eye-catching. I also thought about the medical field because it's more practical, but I still haven't made up my mind. I just need to be more educated, and college is a stepping point to the rest of my life.

When I break away and start my own life, I want to be able to enter my own house or apartment or wherever I'm staying and feel refreshed and be able to relax and study without feeling stressed or crowded by clutter, because that is the way my parents' house makes me feel. I want to be able to have a steady, good job that I like and be successful at it. When I grow up, I still want to know more than even when I graduate from college, if that happens.

It was hard for me to write this story but helpful at the same time. I realized how far I have come as a person and the struggles that my family and I have been through. I'm sure there are many people out in the world with problems like mine—maybe not the same, but struggles in general. My advice to you is find out who you are as a person and never change. Strive for what you believe in and what you want to do in life. Because if you don't, you'll just be stuck in your problems and you won't grow from your mistakes.

"I really want to travel the world a little bit before starting my career, you know, after looking back at my life and how I grew up."

I've Already Come So Far

Most people would love to be rich and powerful, but not me. All I want and hope for from life is a happy and decent living. People always say, "Oh, when I finish college, I'm going to be a great inventor or singer, etc." I'm not one of those people.

This probably sounds like a typical story. And maybe it is at the beginning. I just hope it won't end up like the typical story. Growing up, my family didn't have much. We lived in El Paso, Texas, in government apartments. I was originally born in Phoenix, Arizona, and then we moved to Mexico for the first five years of my life. Then we ended up going to El Paso, where I had a pretty fun and adventurous childhood. I didn't like to hang out with girls because I thought they just talked and weren't very fun. Therefore, I was a tomboy who just had guy friends and I loved to skateboard and do all the stuff that boys did, except I have a younger brother who's just a year younger than me. He also hung around with the same guys I hung out with, and sometimes my friends would rather hang out with him instead because he was a boy. So I went and found myself a few girlfriends who I thought were awesome, and we all became best friends.

Then, my dad got deported to Juarez, Mexico. It was kind of sad, but I didn't worry too much about it because I didn't really understand what was going on. Then, my brothers and I went to Mexico every weekend to visit him. My dad was a drug dealer, and every time we visited him, there were men in the house. At the time I didn't know what they were doing, though I did know he was a drug dealer. He didn't always have money, so sometimes we couldn't eat that day.

After about maybe a year of going back and forth between borders we got some news. It was December a few days before Christmas, and my mom got a call from her sister saying that we should go to Juarez immediately and she couldn't tell us why through the phone. We left for Mexico.

When we got to Mexico, one of my aunts picked us up and took us to our house in Juarez. On our way there, she told us that my father had been murdered. I think most of my family was too shocked or something because me and my sister were the only ones crying at that moment. When we got to our house, there were a lot of police cars and men all around the house. We couldn't go in except for my mom so she could identify the body or whatever. And all I remember hearing was her scream of horror when she saw him on the floor full of blood.

After that, we had a funeral a few days later. We stayed in Mexico for like a week or two, and then we went back to Texas. I was by then in my first year of middle school. (In Texas, you start middle school in sixth grade.) I joined Band because it sounded cool. And that's how my love for music started.

I had a few close friends but not many. My mom didn't know what to do because she couldn't work, and we didn't have much money. We then moved from the apartment we lived in, into some other apartment a few miles away from there. That meant a new school for me. When I enrolled, they asked me if I still wanted to be in Band. I said I didn't want to be in Band anymore, but somehow I ended up in Band anyway. I wasn't happy, and neither were my younger brothers, but we could at least see our friends every once in a while.

After a while of living in our new apartments, my mom decided we were going to move to Omaha, Nebraska. Nobody liked it. Once again, a new school. When I got enrolled again in the new school I was going to attend, they asked me if I wanted to be in Band. I said no, and again I ended up in Band anyway. But before we left to go to Omaha, me and my brothers asked my mom if we could see our friends one last time.

It was a chilly night, and as we approached our friends, there was a certain silence. We played, and we hung out for a little bit. Then it was time to go. My mom was around the corner waiting for us. We hugged our friends and said good-bye. As I got in the van, I realized I probably wouldn't see them again, but there was hope for a better and new life.

When we got to Omaha, I was a little nervous. We didn't know anyone except our aunt and cousins. It was going to be hard to acclimate to this new place, but I had hope. Me and my family lived in my aunt's basement for about six months or so. Then we moved down the street where we were renting a house. I was by then done with seventh grade, I believe. It was summertime, and we were doing pretty well. Things had finally gotten better.

My three aunts, grandma and cousins came to visit from Mexico, and my whole family was pretty excited because we hadn't seen them for a while. They stayed for a while and then they had to leave. They visited us during the summer, so we got to show them around a little bit. We went to the zoo for the first time, and we went swimming. I also made new friends that summer.

Time for school came around, and I was a little nervous and excited. It was my last year in middle school, and then I'd be off to high school. I don't really remember that particular year, but I bet it was because nothing exciting happened, although I did have an art class that I loved. Ever since fifth grade, I've loved having art classes. I just find joy in the simplest things, from drawing a flower to coloring a coloring book. The teacher I had for art class made us explore every different form of art there was, like sculpting, carving, using pastels, water colors and much more. He really helped me discover my love for art and everything that has to do with art.

During the middle of the year, my mom got married to this guy called José. He seemed nice, but I thought, *how could my mom have moved on so quickly?* It really bothered me, but I couldn't do anything about it, so I just moved on with my life and went with it. Them getting married caused us to move from where we were living. That also meant I had to move schools in the middle of the school year. And again I had to enroll, and by this time, I stopped fighting it. I was in Band again. By this time, I was really getting into Band, playing clarinet, and I started liking it. It kind of helped that I was good at it. But I didn't know anyone so I never talked and never made friends. I just waited for the last day of school to come.

And so it came, the last day of school, and I had chopped off the top of my hair. I don't really know why I did it. I just saw that the lead singer of the band Superchick had her hair like that. I thought it looked cool, so I copied her, I guess. So my last day of middle school, I had a fohawk going on, with my long hair on the sides. People complemented me on it, and they thought it was really awesome. But when I got home my sister saw it and she took me right away to a hair salon where they fixed it by cutting off my hair to chin length. I still had a fohawk, but a MUCH better looking one.

Summer ended, and it was time to go back to school. I was really nervous going to high school, like any other freshman would be. The high school I had chosen to go to was South High because most of my friends from my last middle school were going there, and I wanted to see them again. I decided that since I had the power to choose my classes, I would do just that. So my freshman year, I didn't have Band or Art class. Instead, I had JROTC.

Well, it wasn't the best decision I've ever made, I can tell you that. JROTC wasn't what I expected it was going to be. It was boring, and I didn't like it at all. I thought it was going to be more interesting and challenging. As for dance, well, I loved that. I love everything that has to do with or is related with art. But through the second semester our class had a new teacher, and I didn't like her very much. That took away from the experience. By the end of the year, it was time to pick classes for next year. I ended up picking JROTC again because the teacher had recommended me, and I thought that meant you had to do it again. I also signed up again for Band because I missed it and my best friend, Perla, convinced me, too. Ha ha. I didn't sign up for dance or art because I thought high school was the place to explore your possibilities, and that's what I did. School ended, and summer vacations began.

I had wanted to go to Mexico for a while by then, to see my aunts and cousins again. I kept asking my mom if she would send me that summer and she never answered me she just left wondering. But I kept asking and asking, and she said yes, but not until July, for a month. That meant I had to wait 'til my whole summer vacation was basically over to go and only for about four weeks. I couldn't wait. Meanwhile my summer was boring, so I don't really remember much of it. But when it was time to go to Mexico, I was ready to get out. I had to leave by Greyhound bus. It was a long ride. And very boring. It took about a day and a half, but I finally got there. Waiting for me was my aunt, ready to take me to her house. When we got there, my cousins were all waiting outside to greet me with kisses on the cheek. It took me by surprise because I wasn't used to being greeted that way. But I soon got used to it, having to meet so much family. It was a great vacation after all; I got to go swimming and hang out with all my relatives.

Going back to school as a sophomore was a bit different and a lot easier. I knew how to get around school and I knew where everything was. I felt more in control. My first class was Band. That's all I remember from my sophomore year. I've always been a slacker, so I didn't have the greatest grades, and so far I didn't have the credits I needed to be on my way to graduate.

My junior year was very fun and interesting. I had Band again first period. During the summer I got to go to Band camp. I know everyone thinks it's lame and for super Band geeks. But I'd like to contradict you all out there. It was actually very fun and exciting, and now I have memories that can start with "One time in Band Camp..." My second period was Algebra 3-4. My third period was Advisement, or as some people call it, Home-room. My ninth period was Art, and my last period was Physics. That's all I remember from my junior year classes. I never was a planner, so I didn't think of getting the right credits at the time. Boy, do I wish I had done things differently. Towards the end of the year, my counselor started to call me into her office to talk about me graduating. That's when I really started to think more about what I wanted to do with my life and what career I wanted to go with.

I knew what I need to do. I enrolled for summer classes to catch up on all the credits I needed. They were mostly math and science credits. What a surprise, right? Someone struggling with math. Anyway, another school year ended, and I was dreading the thought of having to wake up early while everyone got to sleep in. I went to summer school for about three weeks. I was so relieved when it was finally over. I had like three weeks to relax and kick back before I had to go to Band Camp.

After Band Camp was over, it was time to back to school, and well, here we are now, my senior year. I am so excited be-cause it is finally my last year of high school. This year, I decided to get back into art and music, the things I love doing the most. Like always, my first class is Band, and every morning I look forward to it. My second class is Media Literacy; I'm so glad I am taking this class. I've learned so much about the world and media, and I like learning new things all the time.

My third class is Study Hall, which I use to catch up on my homework and sometimes sleep. My fourth hour is my favorite class of all, Art. I love going to that class everyday because I know that's where I can express myself in a different way, and my teacher always makes me laugh. My fifth class is English with Mrs. Pearson. She's a great teacher. I always have fun in her class. Then it's lunch. Then it's Consumer Math, which I have to take in order to have all the math credits I need to graduate. Then it's Physics for the second time, since I didn't pass it the first time. Finally, I have Algebra because I didn't pass that class the first time, either. I had to learn the hard way that if you want things to happen you have to dedicate yourself to it and STUDY! I'm such a procrastinator. But I'm still working on that. So far I've been seeing my counselor a little more often to talk about college and ACTs and all that good stuff.

I signed up for the ACT and failed to show up because I woke up too late for it. So I'll have to sign up again. I've applied to several colleges, like UNO, Grace University here in Omaha, and Columbia College in Chicago. I am planning on being an undergraduate in fine arts and music. After I graduate, I want to hopefully get married to the love of my life, start a family and start a career as an elementary school art teacher, maybe live in a medium-size house, you know, not too big. Maybe I'll move to Texas to teach there or just stay here. I really want to travel the world a little bit before starting my career, you know, after looking back at my life and how I grew up.

I would have never imagined I'd come so far and accomplish all these things. I mostly wanted to do all these things to show my stepdad that I could do something with my life and be someone (like he said I'd never do). But now, I think I'm actually doing these things for me and because I want to have a better future than most of my brothers and sister, who decided to drop out of high school. All you need to succeed in life is determination and a little bit of hope.

*"At the end of the day
I will close the doors,
enclosing my joy so
it cannot be taken."*

Looking to the Sky for Comfort

The world is harsh. At times, hope leaves and seems like it will not be brought back. With every smile, there is always a tear. With every tear, there is always pain. With escalating pain, hope always leaves.

I awake as the light enters my room, shines upon my face. I lay in bed, feeling as though time has stopped, enjoying the peace of quiet room. A memory overtakes my mind.

The sky is dark. The wind is cold. The only light is from strikes of lightning. Running for shelter, the shadows chase me. I can still feel the cold drops of rain hitting my skin. The chills going down my body. The emptiness of my mind. The thought of not knowing where to go. The tear in my eye that never left.

The memory leaves my mind, and I find myself on my bed. The light is still shining on me, feeling as if time is mine. I jump out of bed, excitement running through my mind.

I jump into my car, not a worry in mind. I now know I have made myself into something. All the long days and nights have paid off. Today, I know I will be doing what I love. I arrive, doors closed, my achievement, my pride, my joy all enclosed in the shop that I own. I open the doors, and a feeling strikes me, throws me into a thought.

Darkness surrounding me, I walk down the street with my feet sore. All I want is to go home, but there is no such place to go. Home to me is a myth. Family is just a word to describe something I don't have. Mom and Dad may not be around, but I do have them, in a place where I am not wanted. A place some call home. So I continue to walk into the darkness.

I get back to my senses. The feeling that struck me has overtaken me. It was not a bad feeling. A feeling of joy because now I am nowhere near my memory. It is just a thought that cannot be reached. The rest of the day I will do what I love. I will work in a place I call my own all day. The time will pass quickly, I won't even notice. At the end of the day I will close the doors, enclosing my joy so it cannot be taken. I get in my car and drive away. I look in my rearview. I see the sun. I feel the power, the energy, the joy of the sun. The magnificent sight of the pink clouds and the sun setting. The blinding rays. Still, I cannot stop staring.

The day was dark. The sky was horrific. The pain was intense, not from the heart but from the mind. Doing my daily routine of high school, a feeling struck me cold, and there were chills climbing up my spine. A horrible feeling came and wouldn't let me go. The panicking would not stop. I had to go home, so there I went … only to find my house robbed and me being the first one to see. Lost and confused, I didn't know what to do. I called my dad. I called the police. An investigator showed up. I looked at him with hatred. To him, I was just another criminal. I didn't let them put me below them. My dad mad. The police judging me. They came to interrogate me. To accuse me. My dad believing every word. They gave a story. They found a conclusion. They accused me. It was not me, but they didn't care. They left; end of story for them. My parents not wanting anything to do with me, their 14-year-old son. They came to a conclusion, the conclusion of hatred. I brought nothing but problems. "Why can't you tell the truth?" they said. I did. But no one listened.

I return to my home, expecting a family dinner. I never had a chance to have a family dinner when I was younger. I never had a functional family before. My family consisted of anger and disappointment. I had never had support of my family or even wanted it. Despite the pain, I will never stop loving them. I grew up pushing everyone away. My heart consisted of so much pain,

I thought I could not handle more. Therefore, I would not let anyone close to me.

As the night ends, I go outside to admire the stars. I climb up to the roof, lay down and gaze at the moon, the same moon that follows me on the long nights, the same moon that has seen me get hurt, the same moon that has been there through all my pain. The world has not changed. The world is still spinning the same way it did when I took my first breath.

Hope is a structure of happiness. Without hope, happiness cannot be. I am seventeen. I cannot say I have made the best decisions. I have pushed people away who I wish I had not. I paid my consequences. Hope has gone from me before. Life has torn me apart, and yet I know my hope is still alive. I won't ever let my hope leave again. Without hope, I will not achieve.

"At my brother's it felt like home, but it wasn't quite home there."

Doing this for You

Fate has brought me here, hate is no option for me, and hope will take over me and make me the best I can be.

Waking up one morning happy as I could be, I was waiting for my mouth-watering breakfast to be cooked and ready to eat. Finished and ready to clean up, I went to the bathroom to shower and get ready for my day to begin. I walked through the kitchen, peeked out the window, and was startled by men dressed in black. They were running around my house, and I was curious why they were doing it. Scared, I went to the door and opened it. Police and a woman from DHS (Department of Human Services) rushed in like it was their own place. The woman questioned my mom about the day earlier, when my little sister got taken away from us. She was home alone, and nobody was watching her. "I blame myself every day; I'm the reason why this all happened," she later said. "I'm the reason she got taken away. I'm sorry for not being there when I was supposed to." Police searched the rest of the house just to make sure it was suitable for kids to live there. Finally, they looked in my parents' room, searched it, and found drugs. It would change my life forever. I never thought I would see my own mother doing drugs, especially meth—probably the worst drug of all. Police asked my mother where she got it, and she gave the answer you get all the time: "It's not mine." I think I know why she said it, maybe just to protect us, so we could all stay together as one family. The police had no questions; they just put her in handcuffs. Then, all the attention went toward my "uncle." My "uncle" was actually my dad, who is in the U.S. illegally. He used my uncle's identification card to have a job and take care of us.

Police saw a family portrait, all three of us kids and my mom and "uncle." My little sister wasn't born yet, so she wasn't in the photo. It was just me, my sister and brother. They took a good look at it, then looked at my mom and "uncle." The police asked, "Why are you in all of these family portraits if you're just an 'uncle'?"

My mom then said, "He's a father figure to the kids, and we're just really close." There my mom went again, trying to lie to the police. It wasn't going to save either her or me and my sisters. Police then put my dad in handcuffs and without saying anything, I saw disappointment and guilt across his face. I got one last hug from my mom and not one good-bye or an "I love you" from my dad. I watched them as they headed to the police car, still disappointed and still guilty. I kept thinking, "Why is he going? He didn't do drugs or anything." I just wanted him to stay. I looked down the street with tears down my face, eyes beet-red, and in a whisper I said, "Good-Bye. I'll miss you and love you forever." The cops grabbed me, told me to get my clothes, and when I walked into my room, I found the couch torn apart, the TV thrown on the floor and clothes all over the place. I grabbed what I could of my stuff and left. Just as me and the cop were leaving, my older sister pulled up and got out of her friend's car. The cop told her to get the stuff she needed because she wasn't 18 or older. She got her stuff and me and her jumped into the car and left. We arrived at Children's Square in Council Bluffs, Iowa, a place where kids go when they have no family to go to. It looked like a prison on the outside—bars on the windows and locks on the fences. We walked inside, and there was my little sister, happy to see me and my older sister. We ate there, slept there, and prayed there every night. Every day, it was like hell sleeping in a room that's not even mine. Every night was a sleepless night. I wanted to break out of there, just go out the front door and make a run for it, but I couldn't leave my family there alone. We stayed there for about a week or so until a woman wanted all three of us kids. We packed our stuff and left with this lady as soon as she got there. She was nice and always smiling, which creeped me out a bit, but I had to deal with it since now I lived with her. When we got to her house, it was dirty with kids all over the place, but I kept my mouth shut. She took my little sister and older sister to their room. I saw only two beds, and I felt scared. Where would I sleep? The nice lady took me to "my" room next. There was a boy in there already. It smelled like sweat and dirt. He had all his stuff on "my" bed. He took it off the bed, and I lay there 'til the next morning. I woke up, eyes as red as could be, no sleep at all. I went to the kitchen and got yelled at by the "nice" lady for looking in a fridge. Why couldn't I even look in a fridge?? What was so bad about that? I walked into "my" room, and I lay there 'til dinner. It came around, and I didn't like what she was cooking so she told me not to eat. I walked in "my" room and lay there once again.

School came along and I was comfortable; it was a way to get away from that house. I made friends who made me really happy. I'd never really had to make friends before; I just always had them. Now it was weird. Later, on the weekends, I would get a chance to go to my friends' houses, and there I took my chance to go see my mom and get some more clothes. Walking into my old house was like entering a cave—dark and gloomy. I found my mother laying in her bed watching TV, tears down her face. She was supposed to be moving out all of our stuff, but all she could do was lay there and cry. I wasn't supposed to be there because the state ordered me not to be around my mother without an adult. I felt bad for her laying there crying. I gave her the last of my money, $80. It was to put gas in the car or for her to get a U-Haul. I gave her a hug and a kiss and left. That night, I thought about it and wondered, "What if she uses that money to buy drugs or something not useful?" I never knew what she did with that money, but she got all of our stuff out of the house, not using her own car or a U-haul. I was so proud of my mom for getting our stuff; she might actually be changing for the better. She put all of our stuff at my grandma's and that was her new "home." After a while, my mom went back on drugs and went to rehab.

Our court date came up, and I was happy. I got to see my mom for the first time in a long time. The judge told my mom she has to go to treatment and have a job to take care of me and my little sister. It was alright for my brother to take us as our foster parent. We went back to the lady's house to get the rest of my stuff and my little sisters stuff. My older sister decided to stay back and graduate early and be out of the system when she turned 18. Now, at my brother's, it felt like a home, but it wasn't quite home there. I needed more, like discipline and to get told if I did something wrong and for someone to tell me what's from right from wrong. My little sister always asked me where mommy was and I paused, tears running down my face. I told her, "She's getting better, and we'll be with her in no time. I promise."

Starting at a new school again was hard the first time, and now it was a second time. It was really hard to get into sports, since I didn't know how anything worked. I worked hard and made the freshman team in basketball. That was the highlight of my freshman year. That kept me going everyday. Going to "my" home and talking about making the basketball team was a good feeling. Just to hear my brother say "good job" made me feel like I could become somebody. Then, sometimes there were bad times going home. Sometimes I would smell the stench of marijuana, and I knew it was coming from the bathroom where my brother was. I thought to myself, *Why put me somewhere just like where I began?* I didn't want to be around drugs anymore; they ruined my life. Every time I smelled that odor, those bad memories would reappear. Drugs don't help anybody in this world. There's no use in them if you're ever going to succeed in life. My mother looked so different after she quit the hard drugs. Her face came back into a good shape, her smile would actually mean something to me, and her hugs and kisses meant something to me. She still cares about her drugs more than her own kids; that's not a mother at all. She does smoke marijuana 'til this day, but I won't be able to change how my mother is nor will anybody else. She's going to make her own decisions, and if that's what she wants to do with her life, then let God take her down her own path. I'm not going to be around that anymore.

Every night when I was away from my mom, I prayed that I could go home. I wish that we could all be together again, but it seemed like it would never happen. I kept thinking God would take me and my little sister where he wanted us to go. I know everyday got closer to us seeing Mom and Dad again. God does a lot of strange things in life, and they happen when they're least expected, but I know in my heart He makes the world a better place and gives everybody a second chance to redeem themselves. My mom needed to get herself together and get herself clean from drugs and get away from the people that she use to hang with. She pushed her way through rehab, and every day, it looked like she got a little bit better. The sun would glow on her face, and you could see her smile so perfectly. It reminded me of that mom I used to have. My mom did her best, and she succeeded in passing rehab. Now all she had to do is get a job and a house, and we'd be home in no time. I would hear from my mom every week about how she would try and get a job. I know it was hard for her to get a job since she was a felon, but I knew she could do it. She got a job at the 24th Street Animal Clinic. We waited everyday, and it got closer and closer to us coming home. I couldn't wait to see her. I say, *Thank you, God, for clean-*

ing my mother of drugs. She could've been in jail or dead, but I'm glad you helped her through it all. God had to give her that little push; that's all. My mom saved up and rented a house that was finally MY home. My little sister and I waited a year and a half for her to get this, and I say, *Thank you, God.* Rehab didn't help at all, though. She still does marijuana, and it's ruining her life and most of all, my little sister's.

These are my hopes and prayers for the future:

God, thank you. Guide my mother through all her rough times, and make sure she is ok for the rest of her life and my family.

I hope my little sister becomes successful and a strong woman.

My older sister, I hope you have fun with your new baby and that it will be healthy and strong, just like you.

Big brother, thank you for all you've done for me. I should thank you every day of my life for teaching me the game of basket-ball. It calms me when I'm down and have no hope in myself, but I push myself to become better and make it big someday. I want to be on that court one day with millions watching me on SportsCenter Top 10 plays. That's my dream, and if it doesn't happen, I'm alright with that because there's so much out there for me to become great in. Thank you for teaching me. I love you.

Dad, thank you for making me a better man and for pushing me to become a successful person in life and not to be a low-life. I go to school every day to make you proud, and I know you're already proud of the choices I've made in life. You're that person who keeps me going, and I know you're going to lead me to the top. Thank you. I love you.

Lacy, you're my whole life. I've never felt like this towards somebody, and I never thought I could be that lucky one to have you. You keep me up when I feel down. When I wake up with you every day, it's like a new adventure. We always have fun, no matter what it is. We can be just sitting there and still make it fun. Thank you most of all. You keep me strong, and I know you're never going to leave my side. You're my best friend and always will be, I promise. Thank you for not giving up on me. I love you, forever. You're my happy ending.

"I would be a liar if I told you I never wanted to be a gangster, or that I didn't want to get revenge, or that I never thought about selling drugs."

El Dolor de Mi Vida
(The Pain of My Life)

Well, first forgive me please if this writing isn't what you expected, and please understand that I'm not a professional writer. Please give me this chance to express myself. So with that said, I would like to say that this is not so you can feel sorry for me or for anybody that has had to face a lot of problems throughout their life. I just want you to know that low income does not mean low intelligence, and I feel it is important for you to try to walk in somebody else's shoes before you judge them. So, as long as I keep hope to overcome adversity, I will not allow myself to become a product of my environment.

I will forever remember the day my father went to prison. It was a sunny day with a nice and cool breeze, the doors were open as well as the windows. My brother and I were playing and running around when my Nana called us into her room. That's when she told us that our father had been sentenced to prison. We were five years old at the time, and it was one month before our sixth birthday. As one might be able to imagine, this was very hard to process: the thought that my father would no longer be a part of my life for a while. Now, that alone was a tragedy, but unfortunately, that wasn't the end. I will get more into detail about that later. My dad was only gone for four years of my life, but those were the most important years of my life. Those were the years when I was most impressionable, the years when I needed someone like my father to look up to and to gain habits that I could carry with me for the rest of my life.

I remember as a kid, my brother and I would be playing and having fun when my brother would start to cry. He cried because he had no dad, and he would say, "I want my daddy, I want my daddy." I would hold him and tell him "It's OK brother, don't worry, it's OK." But I knew inside that it wasn't OK. A coping method my brother used was that he would talk like a baby, and he would call me Dad. Now keep in mind that this is my twin brother, so please excuse my language but that sucked, to have your twin brother call you Dad because he didn't have one. And on top of that, we didn't have our mother.

Before and after my dad went to prison, my mom was really never around, and when she was, she was usually high on meth. My mom was addicted to meth before I was even born, so she really never thought about stopping, even after she had my brother and me. I remember one time my brother and me were sitting in a car, and my mom was outside talking with some girl for a while. I don't remember what they were talking about, but I do remember she opened the back door and gave my brother and me one of those Willie Wonka rope candies, the ones with a red chewy candy in the middle and the small Nerds on the outside. She looked my brother and me in the eye, and she said, "Tomorrow we are going to go to a special place. Do you guys want to go to a special place?" I remember looking into my brother's eyes and seeing the happiest face I have ever seen. The next day my brother and I waited the whole day for her, but she never came for us. We waited on the curb, but she never showed up. To this day, if you tell me you are going to do something for me, I won't hold my breath, because that day I held my breath for so long a part of me died.

Now I'm going to fast-forward a little bit into my early teenage years. My mom was still on dope, and when I was around thirteen, my mom was diagnosed with cancer. When she realized she could possibly die, she started to come around more. She stopped using drugs, and everything was cool. My mom was a strong person. I remember she refused to wear wigs because she wasn't afraid of the facts, and she was ready to face whatever obstacle was put in her way. Then, she was told the cancer was gone after all the treatments (not cured, because once you get cancer, it's never really gone for good). Once it was little-to-nothing, things changed, but not for the good. My mom went back to using drugs. Then, it was back to the old ways ... isolation from the family, anger. I thought once she got back to using drugs, she would never stop, but God must have had other plans for her because she opened her eyes and got sober. Once my mom got sober, things were different. She wanted to be looked at as a mother by my brother and me, which was good, but when you are your kids' friend all of their lives, it's hard to be looked at as a mother. It was good she was sober, but it was harder. I remember when I lived with my mom how rough we had it. My mom was living from paycheck to paycheck. I remember one time she couldn't afford a washer and dryer, so we had to wash our clothes by hand. I would lie down at night and think about how good I had it at my Nana's house.

This whole time I have been talking about how when I was a kid my parents weren't there for me and I had to live with someone else, and that someone was my Nana. When my parents were not there for me, my Nana stepped up to the plate. She made sure I had clothes on my back. Even if they were off-brand clothes, they were clothes. She did live off of welfare, so the fridge wasn't always filled, but my brother and I were always taken care of. As she got older, things got tougher because my brother and I were no angels. We made mistakes and that would stress her out. Even though some of it was our fault, I don't stress too much about it because my Nana wasn't perfect, either. As my brother and I got older, we became too much for her to handle, so she kicked us out, and that day crushed me. She was my father, my mother, and my friend. One thing I'm confused about, though, is that my uncle—her son—was a gang member and he caused a lot of problems, but yet she never kicked him out.

First, let me explain something: my "uncle" is actually my older brother, but when he was born my mom gave him to my Nana, her mother, because my mom felt like she was too young to take care of him. She still wanted to be in his life, so my whole life I called him my uncle. So when I talk about my "uncle", he is really my brother. My uncle, at a young age, felt like he needed to belong, so he joined a gang. And since he lived with me, I saw everything he did—how he treated women, how he sold drugs, how to hold a gun, and the list goes on. I held a gun for the first time before I was a teenager, and I smoked weed before I was a teenager. Due to the choices my uncle made, our house was shot at a couple of times. When you walk into your house and you can see the outside because of the bullet holes in the walls, well, that's something that gives you a feeling you can't even imagine, and because we didn't have a lot of money, we couldn't fix the walls. I would be liar if I told you I never wanted to be a gangster, or that I didn't want to get revenge, or that I never thought about selling drugs. At one point in time, I did want to do all these things, but God let me see hope when there was no hope in sight.

In my belief, God created everything, and he sent his only son to earth so he could die for my sins. I pray to God because too many times, I should have been six feet under. But for some reason—some *purpose*—God kept me alive. I believe God has a plan for me, and he will never give me an obstacle that I can't overcome. I have this quote that I live by, and somebody told me this, but I switched the words around and I made it my own: "God gave me a chance to <u>represent</u> myself, and if I make mistakes, I won't be afraid because God will give me a chance to <u>re-present</u> myself." This is a big part of why I am who I am.

116

Even with my house being shot at and raided, I still managed to meet great men like Beto Gonzales, the gang counselor who works out of the Boys and Girls Club, and Wes Hall, a motivational speaker who frequently visits my school, who would forever have a huge impact in my life. These two men have educated me on life and have been like father figures to me. Even with struggles like not much food in the fridge and even not having a mom or dad for a long period of my life and having bullet holes in the walls of my house, I have always kept an optimistic mentality, and for that, I thank God. He gave me hope when I didn't think there was any, and thanks to my God, my family is doing a lot better than when I was a kid. My mother has stopped using drugs, and my father and I have been able to build a relationship. I'm looked at as a powerful young man in my community; I'm going to graduate high school and go to college.

Hopefully, now you understand that low income doesn't mean low intelligence, and you should walk into somebody else's shoes before you judge them. If you ever forget that, think of me. I could have easily become a gangster or a nobody because of my obstacles, but I'm not.

"I want to be the person to find out who actually committed the crime."

My Future

Goals. Everyone has at least one goal for the future. People have to go through struggles and difficulties to reach them; they don't come easy. For example, family or financial problems get in the way of many goals. People tend to put their families before themselves, putting their goals on hold, and after a while, they just don't have the drive to pursue it any longer. Financial issues also get in the way of people reaching their goals. What they have to realize is that you don't always need money to accomplish or reach a goal. I have a goal for the future. I know it won't come easy, but I am willing to do whatever it takes. I want to improve my community by going to school and studying criminal justice/forensics to help investigate and solve crimes.

Many people have other people in their lives or things that may inspire them. No one thing or person in particular inspired me, it was many things. What really got my attention first was the show *CSI: Miami*. CSI stands for Crime Scene Investigation. From the very first episode I watched a few years ago, I was hooked, even though I knew it was not real. However, a lot of the stuff they do in the show is how it is done. The show starts with the crime, to grab your attention. It then rewinds and shows all the steps of investigation. They interview suspects, victims, and witnesses. At the end, they finally put the puzzle together and find out exactly what happened. There have been a couple of CSI episodes that never really told us the conclusion. They left us with the suspense of wondering who it could have been. That is when I like it the most, because then I become a CSI, just for that moment.

Crime novels also grab my attention. I read mostly novels that were based on true events. For example, *Snitch* and *Street Pharm*. They are both about the drug industry and gangs. I enjoy reading them because they give me a chance to try and solve the crime before I get to the end of the book. Everything I read leads up to the case and what happened. By the end of the books, I realize if my analysis was right or not. This is my motive. Because if I was wrong, I go back and look to see what part I mistook and didn't pay close enough attention to.

In Texas, I witnessed something that I wish I never would have seen. What I saw was not something you see or experience every day. I remember it as if it just happened. My family and I were on our way back from our three-week vacation in Mexico. Our vehicle needed gas, so we got off the highway to get some at the gas station. As we proceeded off the ramp, we saw a man collapse in the middle of the street. At first, I thought he just fainted. As we stopped, we realized he wasn't moving. We saw blood through his white shirt. Once I saw that, I freaked. I didn't know what to do. I was in shock. I was sad, worried, and scared for the man. I didn't know if he was dead or alive. My little brother and sisters were in the vehicle and my parents did not want them seeing that, so we drove off. Seeing that made me love and appreciate my family so much more. It made me realize how fast things can happen, in a blink of an eye. I knew I wanted to be a CSI, but this? *This* was my drive toward forensics and investigation, even more.

The death of my cousin Andy also motivated me to be an investigator. The way things went down was odd and confusing. It all began because my cousin missed his car ride to South Dakota, where he was going to go visit family. He was getting off the bus when a car stopped next to him. A woman got out of the car and began to argue with Andy. I wasn't close with Andy, but my family told me he didn't like problems and confrontation; he minded his own. He argued back for a bit, but then he walked away. As my cousin turned to walk away, the man who was driving the car shot Andy. Andy fell to the ground and the man shot him two more times. Immediately, they drove off. It still has not been established why the woman was arguing with my cousin. They have not begun the trial yet. As of right now, she is being charged with accessory to murder, while the man is being charged with second-degree murder. The death of my cousin affected my grandma and my uncle. The loss itself killed them inside. But for them to know who did it and not be able to do anything about it was what really got to them.

The death of my cousin motivates me to pursue this career because as a CSI, you need to find out what specifically happened. In this case, there are about three different stories. I want to be a CSI who finds the ONE specific and accurate story. Growing up, I remember family members always talking about "Mr. B," who is my mom's brother. All I knew about him was that he was my uncle and he was in prison. Throughout the years, I still didn't really know much about him. I would see how much it affected my family and how they would cry when he came up in conversations. When I turned fifteen, I asked my mom about him. She told me that she thought I was finally mature enough and ready to know about what had happened. We sat down at the kitchen table. She began to tell me why he was there. It was then that I felt the pain that I had seen my family feel all those years. It finally hit me. I started crying; all my emotions came out. My uncle is in prison for life due to murder. This part of my story is not for sympathy, but to show why this part of my life was yet another thing driving me toward forensics. My uncle never really hung out with the brightest group of kids. He hung out with all the mischievous troublemakers. My uncle saw that he wasn't going to get anywhere hanging out with those kids, so he moved to Chicago. Shortly after, my grandma convinced him to move back to Omaha. He kept in touch with his childhood friends and as soon as he got back, they got together. One night they were at a party and decided to retaliate against one of their rival gangs, due to the fact that the rivals killed one of his friends. My uncle and his friends hijacked one of the guy's vans. They never really planned on killing him, but they did. They dropped the dead body in the streets and the van in the Missouri River.

My uncle and one of the other guys were charged with first-degree murder, while the other three men were charged with second-degree murder. So, these guys are supposed to be my uncle's friends, right? I mean, they grew up together, they never lost touch, they were "brothers." That all changed. His friends went against him and put all of the blame of him. My uncle isn't even the one who actually committed the crime. He didn't pull the trigger. My uncle is now spending life in prison, while his friends are free. As I am writing this and talking to my mom about it, she tells me that the day my uncle got arrested, he had just dropped off diapers and formula to her for me. I was just two months old at the time. My mom said he gave me a kiss on my forehead, and said "I love you, Mija!"

My uncle's case is my main drive toward forensics. I want to be the person to find out who actually committed the crime. I don't want someone doing all that time if they really didn't commit the crime. The person who committed the crime needs to be the one behind bars. A person shouldn't have to be miserable for the rest of their lives if it was not them.

I have high hopes for my future. I will graduate from Omaha South High Magnet in May of 2011 with honors. As of now, I am ranked 33 out of 333 students in my graduating class; I plan to keep that rank, if not move up even higher. I am in the application process for college now. I have applied to multiple schools, and I am still not done applying. I have a few schools looking at me for volleyball. We'll see how that goes, but I am more focused on my career. In ten years, I see myself with a steady job as a CSI. I can see myself reaching my goal because I am a very driven person. I work hard for what I want and the person I want to become. With the help and motivation from my family and friends, I know I will make it, especially with all the help from my parents. I love you!

"*My brother and sister had not a thing to eat. Nothing.*"

The 10 Minutes that Changed My Life

It was the summer of 2006, and I had barely moved to Omaha, Nebraska, from Ohio. Sixth grade was just the beginning for me. That morning, I walked into class not knowing anyone. I sat in the desk quietly; usually, that is not me. Once the week passed by, I got the chance to meet this really nice girl. At first, she seemed like a show-off, but time proved me wrong, and up until now, the year 2010, she still is being a really nice girl and is my best friend.

One morning during sixth grade, I woke up with the worst pain ever in my stomach. I couldn't even look at food or anything that had to do with eating. To me, everything tasted nasty. Later that day, I got sent home and went straight to my room. I remember crying all day. I could not stop crying from the pain. I stayed home for one full day with the pain. On a scale of 1 to 10, it was a 40!!!

The next night, my mom decided to take me to the hospital, and I spent the night there because the next day at seven in the morning, I was going to go in for an operation to remove my appendix. I stayed there for one week, and I even spent Valentine's Day at the hospital. My mother had to stop working so that she could stay with me at the hospital. At my house, no one else worked but my mom. My brother and sisters went to school. When they would visit me, they seemed sick. Why? Well, I'll tell you why. We didn't have any money, not even for food. My dad didn't live with us, so my mother was the only one who supported my house. My brother and sister had not a thing to eat. Nothing.

After a week of being in the hospital, I finally got to go home. That didn't mean I felt good. I was still in pain. I had a tube inside my stomach, which I finally got removed three weeks later. Sixth grade was over. I graduated from sixth grade.

That summer, I went to summer school, but not for long. I stopped going because I would go to work with my mom instead at a hotel doing housekeeping. We had a great time. I got my first paycheck; it was for $178.63! Yes, I know. I still remember. I still remember because it was my money that I had earned with my own sweat. My whole summer I spent working and having some good times. More work, then more good times, and then my summer was over. Middle school was just weeks away from starting.

My seventh grade of school was crazy. I became more of a troublemaker attitude girl. One thing I did well was to keep good grades up in all my classes, especially science. My teacher was such a monkey ... ha ha! Monkey was the word I used instead of cussing. My math class was the best class ever because the class was all about laughing so hard, always having the best time of the day. With all the crazy things I did, I'm still surprised I passed on to eighth grade.

For me, eighth grade was worse because my mother and I didn't get along. We had differences and were not always on the same page, if you know what I mean by that. There were times when I would have to tell my mom where I was going after school. If she called me, I never answered my cell. Basically, I never cared about what the family said. I was always being a brat about everything. I even skipped and wouldn't even come back until I thought it was the right time to come back from school. Always with the smart talking. And that's just the way things were every day.

At the end of the year, graduating from middle school was an accomplishment I made for myself. When my graduation came, I was sitting down in a chair, getting ready to receive my diploma. I looked around to see if any of my family members came, and guess what? No one from my family showed up. That hurt me, but I guess that was my fault for being the way that I was with my family. That day, I received my eighth grade diploma. I walked home crying, knowing that I had no support from any of the people I loved.

High school came. That summer, my sister was four months pregnant. The pregnancy changed the way I was with my mom. It made me see things differently. I became more of a responsible person. My sister's pregnancy was risky. When she was four months pregnant, she found out that the baby was having problems. My sister found out that my niece would not survive. Either she would die during her pregnancy or after my niece was born. They gave her options of aborting the baby or to keep going with the pregnancy. But my sister, of course, kept going with the pregnancy, even though the baby was having problems. Months went by, and my niece was born. She was only alive for ten minutes. Her body was not normal. Her lungs and all her organs were outside her body, and her bottom was on the front of her body instead of at the back. One of her arms was smaller than the other one, and the same for her little toes of her feet. Some of her fingers were even stuck together. It made me realize that you have to be different and give people respect if you want to get respect. It made me see that you should admire people for who they are and never judge them. It made me grow up.

In high school now, I have always worked for my own things, and I have always bought things for myself. It got to a point where I begged my parents to buy me a car, but of course, they never did. So I bought myself my own car by working and earning my own money, and I finally earned enough money to buy me a 1998 Yukon. I paid $1,300. To me, it seemed pretty cheap, so I thought, why not buy it?

Now I am a senior. One of my top classes is JROTC because this class has made my personal ways change and made me a stronger person who is able to give myself respect. After I graduate, I would like to attend Iowa Western to study Criminal Law and Justice. My backup plan would be to join the Air Force. At this point in my life, I am willing to do anything that I can to be a successful person.

Even though I've been through a lot in my life, losing someone I loved who meant a lot to me, yelling at my mother, going to high school and realizing that life goes on—with or without a support system—I am always trying to give the best of myself and keeping my head up.

At a young age, I went through a lot of pain, and now that I am older, I see things differently. I see myself more grown up. No matter what problems I go through, I won't let those things get in my way of who I want to be in life.

A message for someone out there in the world would be: don't let anyone or anything get in your way. If you don't get along with a family member, try to do your best to change that. Always give the best of yourself and prove to people and your loved ones that you're brave enough to do and be who you want to be in this world. One more thing: keep communication with the ones that have been there the most for you. If I can do it, you can, too.

"My grandparents told me that the bullies weren't worth it, that they were the ones who felt bad about themselves, which is why they were picking on me."

What Presides Within

My seventeen-year long life has lobbed many obstacles my way. I have pulled through many struggles. These struggles shaped me for who I am today. There were many times that I was down, and I couldn't help but think: Would my grandparents want me to be like this? No, they definitely would not! They would tell me to pick myself up, jump back up on that horse, and smile at that sunshine.

My past isn't the most astounding subject in my life, but I've learned a lot from most of my negative experiences. Everyone has bad experiences and memories in their life. It is inevitable. I merely had to learn to clear away the fog and take in the beautiful sunshine that is splayed in the sky. They've shaped me into who I am today.

I have also had a lot of positive experiences that I reflect upon today. I reflect on these experiences with utmost happiness.

My grandmother and grandfather, Marie and Howard, adopted me and my sister, Amber. I was three and Amber was two when our parents divorced. My mother filed for divorce because my father verbally and physically abused my sister and myself. She just couldn't take it anymore, and they both filed for divorce. My sister and I were then adopted by our grandparents, who loved us dearly, just as much as we loved them. Our father was allowed to visit us every now and then, along with our mother. (They both visited at different times. Lord forbid them coming on the same date!) My sister and I loved it when they would visit because we definitely missed them and because of the gifts they bought us. (Sadly, we looked forward to the gifts more so than actually seeing them because, well, we loved toys!)

Our grandparents raised us well. They definitely knew how to raise children with devotion, love, and unwavering care. They also knew how to punish us fairly, especially when we did not eat our peas and carrots. Every day as a child was beautiful, fun, and vivid. Amber and I would play in the front yard with cheer and playfulness. Those days were the best, with butterflies fluttering and our shoes padding along the soft, rich grass. I would give a lot to go back to those wonderful, vivid days. I know I learned the most when I was a child rather than in school.

Then, I blossomed into my teenage years and started junior high. I learned the most as a child—don't get me wrong—but I have also learned a lot as a teenager. My best friend ever since kindergarten stuck by me all these years and we couldn't be separated; we were so much alike. My self-esteem certainly was low due to the fact that many people made fun of me. Of course I had my friends, but the hurt inside from all those people eventually built up and I didn't want to go to school anymore. It had gotten to the point that I wanted to commit suicide. I felt like a useless heap in the world, and I felt like I would be doing the world a favor by taking my own life. My grandparents told me that the bullies weren't worth it, that they were the ones who felt bad for themselves, which is why they were picking on me. They told me to forget whatever the bullies told me. Most importantly, my grandma and grandpa told me that I was really important and that I had a marvelous sense of humor. At this point, I realized that they were right and that by smiling and laughing I could get through this bullying stage. I also realized that I wasn't paying attention to my good buddies, who were so important to me. I almost let the bullying consume my life. But with the help of my ecstatic friends and caring grandparents, I pulled through. I personally believe that the bond between friends can be one of incredible strength and force. You feel so good when you know that you have someone that you can discuss personal matters and problems with—someone to express yourself to, someone that will be there for you through all the clutter.

After I graduated from junior high, I went on to high school. It's funny because all of my buddies planned on going to Central High School; but to no avail. I was the only who went there. All my other friends' parents wanted them to go somewhere different, and we were all separated. That wasn't according to the plan.

The summer before I started high school, my grandparents both died due to horrible third-degree strokes. Marie T. Morgan, my beloved grandmother, died at the beginning of summer, whereas Howard died near the end of summer. The sadness that was bestowed upon my heart was of incredible force. I couldn't concentrate on my schoolwork because of that draining sadness. I failed all my classes first semester.

But alas! Then came second semester, and I gained a great friend by the name of Ian House. To be frank, he was my rock. He told me to pick myself up and get going with my life. He said to have fun because that's what my grandparents would want.

Have fun is what he told me to do, and that is definitely what I did. I started to skateboard around the neighborhood, taking in the breeze as I descended the angled slope of the hill. Whenever I skateboard, this rush of energy comes into me, and it feels good. Instead of mourning over the sadness of my loss, I had fun. I personally believe that instead of looking upon losses negatively, why not look upon them positively? Yes, the loss was a hard blow, but it did me no good to look upon their deaths negatively. Pondering on anything too negatively is dangerous to anyone, in my opinion.

I got on the ball and passed all my second semester classes with flying colors. The teachers loved me, and I am so appreciative of the knowledge they bestowed to me. I never really took into account how we all don't give enough gratitude toward teachers. Even though I passed all my classes second semester, I definitely didn't have enough credits to become a sophomore. So, I then had to stay for summer school. I got some of the same teachers, which surprised me somewhat and was a good thing. I picked up all my credits, and that summer was one of the best summers of my life.

I transferred schools to South High because during that awesome summer, I met a girl by the name of Chelsea, and she demanded for me to come to South High. I juggled it around in my mind for about a week and then I told her yes, since I knew a lot of people there anyway.

I started at South, and I love the teachers and the building. It's way easier to navigate than Central. The curriculum was of good nature, and I got the most out of all the electives. Currently, I'm a senior and two weekends ago, I went to a camp called Inclucity. The camp consisted of four Omaha area schools: South, North, Northwest, and Millard North. It's a camp that changed my perspective on the way I treat myself and everyone around me. Within a weekend, I learned so much about myself and the way I treat others around me. It taught me to strive for community alliance and to try my best in trying to make this world a better place by fighting discrimination and other forms of hate. I have joined in with the Unity Club at school because I believe that unity is very important. Truly, Inclucity brought out the better in me.

I applied online to the University of Nebraska-Omaha and to Metro Community College, and I hope that UNO accepts me. I plan on becoming a commercial pilot, and through UNO's great aviation program, that goal could be within my reach. Ever since childhood, I wanted to become a commercial pilot and (you betcha!) I still do. My life is only getting started, and (guess what, Grandma?) I'm smiling at that sunshine that's splayed right in front of me. The future will lob even more obstacles before me, and I will take on the challenge.

Family: Parents & Grandparents

"I needed to start working even harder than before – both mentally and physically. I knew that would be my motivation."

Still Growing, Still Deciding

My mom is the reason why I want to be successful. She is what inspires me to do better. She has shown me that no matter how tough things get, we have got to keep on pushing forward, and that makes my mother a woman of strong character. She is the type of women that once you think she's going to break and quit, she gets right back on her feet. I think that what has pushed her through the struggles in her life has been hope, so I want to learn to hope like she does.

My mother has had a big impact in my life. She has taught me that quitting is never the answer or the way out. I guess that's the reason why I hate losing. When I set my mind on something, I have to achieve it, and if for any reason I don't achieve what I've set myself to achieve, it becomes my obsession. I won't stop until I have gotten the goals I've set out for. My mind is set on giving my mom everything she has always wanted; I'm not going to stop until I do so.

I might be a little self-motivated, but mostly it is my mother who is the motor in me. Sometimes I think how things would have been different if I were trying to go to school, keep myself on track and make a better person of myself for someone else or another reason. I think I wouldn't be on the same path. I don't think I would be working as hard. The will to succeed comes from wanting to make her proud. That's a force I feel inside me that I can't explain.

I lived with my mother in Zamora, Michoacán, Mexico. I used to go to school for a half day every day, going to work after school. The fields were big, and they were used to grow crops such as corn, strawberries and wheat. The work was hard, the hours were long, and halfway during the day, it would get really hot. I would think about just getting that day over and onto the next one. My thoughts were always "The more money that I make, the more I can help my mother and myself." I actually liked the way things were going, but then my mother approached me and said, "Do you want to go to the U.S.?" I remember not wanting to go, but I still came. The reason why I think didn't want to come was because I thought my mom needed me there. I didn't want to leave her alone. Most of all, I think I was scared of the change, how this would affect me.

I started high school as a freshman. I never wanted to be here. I would start fights, talk back to some teachers and just be plain-out rude. Everything I was doing was an effort to get sent back to Mexico with my mom. My mother told me that there was no way I was going to be sent back, that this was the place I needed to be. My mother is a very sage woman, and she was right that South Omaha was where I needed to be.

I was never really sure what or who I wanted to be in life until I attended an architectural expo in town. It was at the Qwest Center. I didn't want to go, but my family said, "Come on, let's go. You might find it interesting." I remember seeing this man at a booth with a small model that seemed weak. He told me that he could stack twenty books on this model. I didn't believe him, so I told him I wanted to see. I was hoping that it would break and he would be embarrassed. He started stacking big book after book until he reached twenty books. He told me I could stack more, but those were all he brought with him. I was amazed. He looked at me and smiled. He said the key is to have a good base to withstand anything. From that day on, I knew that architecture was something I wanted study.

That is, until I started writing my essay for this project. Suddenly, I went from thinking that everything I did was for my mom to realizing that I would have to do it for me. It doesn't seem like a lot, but once you've been doing something for so long, it doesn't seem and feel right when you want to change it. It was very difficult for me, and I felt so unfocused. I didn't know what was going on. The transition was hard, but I managed to get through it. A very wise and smart man named Will said to me, "We have to do things for ourselves even if it sounds selfish." I had a very hard time getting over this. I struggled trying to focus. I had trouble doing simple things, even like just taking a shower, putting on my clothes, and cooking. I had so much trouble trying to stay focused that one morning I was making myself some eggs, and I burned them—and it wasn't a little bit, either. I would think about what was going on inside my head. I would have random thoughts about my mom, my family, the way I used to work, and the things that I enjoyed doing with my friends. These thoughts would come in the weirdest moments; I would be at the gym and have thoughts about how hard I used to work and that this felt like nothing. I guess I was missing all of these things. I would write all these things down. I realized that I'm a person who always wants to improve and not go back. I felt like I wasn't improving because I wasn't working as hard as I used to, that I was taking it easy on myself, and that I needed to start working even harder than before—both mentally and physically. I knew that would be my motivation.

I started looking at different careers, like how to be a boxing coach. Boxing is difficult sport both to do and to teach. To be a boxing trainer, you need have experienced the sport first hand. To be qualified, you need to win a couple Golden Glove tournaments and have fought in a certain number of pro matches. It takes a lot more than what people actually think. I also went and toured some cooking schools and their programs. The people at the schools gave me a tour of their kitchens. I was amazed by their facilities. Metro Community College has a very big kitchen with a lot of new appliances, such as stoves, boilers and also refrigerators. I went to this engineering firm called Engineering Technologies, Inc. It was a small place, but it had a lot of things, such as pictures of buildings they had designed, things they had made, and they also had a very interesting sculpture in the entrance, something that is very unique and made out of a lot of different materials. It had a lot of covers, twists and turns. Although it didn't have much color, it still brightened up the room.

Sometimes, we just we need a little push or good words to motivate us and get ourselves back on track. Now I have my motivation back, but I'm still not sure who or what I want to be. All really know is that I want to become a better person and improve until I achieve something that is worthy of all my hard work.

"All her hard work makes me want to work as hard as she did, but to have better success than she had. I want to make her proud."

My Mom's Hands

My mom has the hands of a person who has worked hard her whole life. Her hands are rough, cracked, and calloused. They have suffered and worked a lot, and now she suffers because they hurt a lot. Her dream was to be a hairstylist and she wanted to own her own beauty salon. She also wanted to be a kindergarten teacher and teach where she went to kindergarten. I think she would have been a good teacher because she likes little kids. She had a lot of sisters and was the second of five girls. They had one brother. Her mother was very caring but made her kids work a lot. Her father was never there for them and was always drinking and gambling. He'd rather help the neighbors than his own children. They would always protect the boy because he'd always try to get in trouble with bigger kids.

When my mom was nine years old, she started working at her dad's leather shop. She and her sisters had to help out every morning before they went to school. She says she didn't have a normal childhood because she worked a lot. Her hands were always dirty and covered in paint and leatherwork, so she always hid her hands. Her parents didn't have the money to put her through school, so she dropped out in the ninth grade to help support the family.

The first time she came to the United States, she was sixteen. Somehow, she snuck in, but she went back home after a short while. She was running away from a marriage proposal; she felt she was too young to get married. She asked her parents about it and they said it was her decision whether she would get married or leave and study. She chose to leave.

The second time she came to America, she was twenty-five years old and it was around November when she crossed the border with my older sister. She found out later that she was pregnant with me while she was crossing. She was running away from my dad. He was a drug dealer, and she never wants to talk about him. Mexico was hard for her, and she needed to get money. Like everyone else, she wanted to realize the American Dream and to have a better life for herself and her children. She had a horrific experience during the crossing. She had no food or water and had to walk or run for eighteen hours. She was trying to avoid immigration officers and had to hide in bushes for a while, sometimes hours, as the officers came by. It took her two days to finally get to San Pedro, California. When she got there, she learned of her pregnancy. None of her sisters who lived in California wanted her to live with them because they thought we would be a burden on them, so she ended up in a shelter for a while.

Mom had to raise four kids – three boys, one girl – for seven years by herself. She worked hard every day, babysitting, at thrift stores, and at meat packing plants. She would leave at two in the afternoon and come home at two in the morning. Recently, my sister got into trouble. She went over to Mexico to visit family, and while she was over there, she decided to visit our dad. She was going from one part of Mexico to another with him, and police found drugs in the car. She is now in jail and so are my dad and two other people who were in the car. She has a lawyer and is trying to get out. My dad won't confess that they were his drugs. My mom was really angry at my dad because he got on his knees and begged my sister to take the blame. She was mad at my sister for not thinking right about what she was doing. She knew he was bad, a drug dealer, but she still went to see him after all that he had done. Everyone from his family is on my sister's side, all his brothers and uncles, and they're testifying for her in court.

Getting her immigration papers was another time of great

suffering for my mom because she had to go to Ciudad Juarez, Mexico, for an interview to see if she qualified to get her papers. This was about two years ago. She left all of us here to do this. When she got there, she found out that she didn't qualify at the time, because she needed a pardon or waiver for crossing illegally the first time. She had to wait there for three months to get everything she needed and then tried again to see if she qualified. She wasted a lot of money on the papers, but she said that what she really lost the most was spending that time away from her kids and missing Christmas with us. Life was hard for us without her because we were used to having her there.

Eight years ago, my mom got married again and had my little brother. My mom has her papers now, and so does he. Her hard work gave her a happy ending. She is talking about going back to school to become a hairstylist and to realize her dream, finally. She is my hero. All her hard works makes me want to work as hard as she did, but to have better success than she had. I want to make her proud. I want her to see that her hard work actually did pay off. She always wanted me to get a good education so I wouldn't end up having to struggle the way she did, working at packing plants and other bad places. She didn't want me to go to Marines because it's dangerous, but she wants me to go to college, get an education and a good job.

My dream is to join the Marines and then train to become a professional UFC fighter because I've always liked fighting, ever since I was little. It helps release my stress. In ten years, I will have my money, my house, and most importantly buy a big house and cars for my mom. I will have a wife and kids, and hopefully no mushroom ear from all the fighting. I want to be one of those fathers who goes to his kids' soccer games, supports his kids a lot, not necessarily spoiling them but giving them everything they need. I want my kids to know how to be good fathers and mothers who don't bail on their kids or family, like my father did. I want to teach them responsibility when they are young and that hard work pays off and how to take care of what they have. I don't want them to take anything for granted. I will tell them about my parents, that my father was a bad man, but that's it about him. I will tell them that my mom is my hero, the person who got me through life. She's the best mother in life. She's the most hardworking person I know. I will tell them what her hands look like, because they symbolize hard work. She works harder than any man would work, and her hands show it. I want my hands to look like hers someday.

"Growing up, I haven't had the person I really needed. That would be my mom."

Maná Olana

Family should be a big part in everyone's life. They are in mine. They have set bad and good examples for me to learn from. Good examples are like going to college and making something out of their lives. They have always made sure that I stay focused in school and that I get good grades. They always check up on my grades to make sure my grades are good.

In soccer, they do the same thing. I've been playing since the sixth grade, so I love playing, and they have always loved watching. I started playing because my friend's dad made a team and asked me to play. I sucked at first. I couldn't do anything with the ball; it was funny. Even though I wasn't good, my family was there supporting me. Now I play club and varsity for school in the spring, and they are still there to support me. I grew up playing with my oldest brother and two cousins. We still all play together when we get the chance. My grandma and aunt make sure I show up to every practice and game. My aunt makes sure to take me to practice and games. She always stays and watches, too.

Growing up, I haven't had the person I really needed. That would be my mom. When I was in sixth grade, she went away to prison. Having to grow up and going to visit my mom somewhere I shouldn't ever have to go was hard. The long drive to Texas was hard. It took so long. Saying bye was even harder. Knowing I had to leave and drive all the way back to Omaha was harder. The first couple of times were emotional. I hated going there. We would stay and visit for up to six hours, so that wasn't as bad. As I grew up and her time there got shorter, it got easier for me to accept.

Physically, she hasn't been in my life that much. She hasn't been there when I needed her the most. That would be my teenage years. It's hard not having someone as close as my mother to talk to. Not having her in person or at the moment makes things a little tougher to get through. Even though she's not here, I can talk to her about my problems, and she's always there to listen. I do talk to her a lot on the phone, which makes things better. We can always make each other laugh. In the letters she would write me, she would always write a quote on the back to keep my head up. That quote was "Don't let your chin touch your chest," and still today, I follow that quote.

My mom and I have always had a good mother-daughter bond. She has always made sure we have support in everything. She makes sure my family is always there for me. Even though we haven't had her, in my book she's still a good mom. Not once in my life have I ever wished for a different mom.

I think it's not as hard not having her because I have my grandma. She is the most important person in my life. She is a big part of the way I am today. The stories she has told me about my mom and aunts and uncles are for me to learn from. Like them getting into trouble with their friends. Since I was a little girl, I have been close to her. She had seven kids and despite being so old, she has raised me and my two brothers, as well. I understand it's hard for her. It's not easy raising a nine-year-old and two teenagers, but she has all these years.

She does get sick, and it worries us a lot. Somehow, she always ends up getting better. At first, it was her and my grandpa that watched us. My grandpa passed away and left her alone to watch me and my oldest brother. By seeing her, I could tell it was tough and stressful. She thought she couldn't do it. She has up until now. I don't know what I would do without her. We have a good bond, and I don't ever want to lose that.

A memory I have with my grandma is going to Hawaii. It was the summer before sophomore year. Going somewhere that far away and so nice was something I will always remember doing with her. Two of her kids live there, so I know she loves going there. Her taking me was not something every grandma would do. It meant a lot to me. We had so much fun there. We would go to the beach every day. Shopping, dinner and driving around the island were amazing. Doing all that with my grandma was even better.

If it wasn't for my grandma, my oldest brother and I probably wouldn't be so close. We fight a lot, but every brother and sister fight. As weird as it sounds, that's how we get along. We make each other laugh and make each other mad, but I don't know what I would do without him. We have always gone through the same tough situations, like my mom going away and my grandpa dying, so we have always had each other. We have always understood each other, so it's nice having him in my life. He has a good future set out for him. He wants to get done with college and be a cop. I hope he comes through with what he wants to do later on in life.

I also have a little brother and two little sisters. My brother lives with me, but my sisters don't. My little brother is a smart little boy. He is very involved with sports in school. He has played baseball and was pretty good. Now he's trying soccer, and he's not bad.

I don't see much of my little sisters. They have a different mom. They live with my dad, so when I go visit him, I see them. They are so cute. Even though I don't see them as often as I would like, that doesn't change anything. Even though we're not always around each other, they look up to me. I think it's because I'm their oldest sister. They would much rather be around me than my older brother. When I go over and visit, I make sure to spend all my time with them. I love that they look up to me because they mean a lot to me. I want them to grow up and be role models for each other.

Another person who I'm really close to is my little cousin Mariah. I try to be a good role model for her, too. She's a sophomore in high school, and I know it's hard getting around all the negative things and staying focused in school. I was a sophomore two years ago. She is also going to go through the experiences I had to go through with friends—drinking, smoking, and all the bad influences out there. I think if she does what I did and tries her best to stay focused in school and hang around the right crowd, she will be fine. Sometimes, it's going to seem like her friends or boys are more important than school. It might seem that way, but it's really not. Friends are not always going to be there. I just really want her to stay focused now so that later on in her high school years she has nothing to worry about.

My mom got pregnant at 15. She has told me how hard it was, making me think twice about my decisions. My two cousins have gotten pregnant at 18. They have also told me how hard it was. They said it's hard being a teenager and a mother. So hearing it from all three of them has given me an idea of how hard and stressful it might be. I hope that just like I have learned from my mom and my cousins, Mariah will, too. I have many hopes for her. I want her to follow my path in a way. I want her to set goals for herself. A big thing I want her to do is stay away from bad influences like I have.

My aunt from Missouri is like my best friend. I can be totally open and honest with her about everything. She gives me advice on everything about life. She tells me like it is. Even though she only comes into town every three weeks, I can always depend on her. She knows it's hard being a teenager. She understands peer pressure or just getting tempted to do things when you're around your friends. She gets me in every way. I think she's a really good role model. She is always there for her family and even though

I'm not her daughter, she goes out of her way to get me what I need. I look up to her a lot.

I'm close to graduating. I want to get done with high school, and I plan on going to college after. After graduation I plan on going to Hawaii to spend time with my family there that I barely see. I'm really close to my cousins there, and even though we live so far away, we make sure to keep in touch. I have many good memories in Hawaii with my family there. The beach with my cousins is something I will never forget. It's a beautiful place to spend time with family. After college is done, I want to spend a lot of time with my mom. I want to catch up on each other's lives. I think that is very important. When I'm settled in with school and my mom, I want to focus more on my life. After my career is on the right path I want to get married and have a family. I think that's what every girl wants. I want my kids to have a good future and I want my family's examples to be a part of their lives, so they learn from them just like I did.

Without the family I have, I probably wouldn't be the person I am now. I wouldn't have my grandma inspiring and pushing me to do what I have so far. I think family should be a big part of everyone's life. No matter what, you can always count on them. They should always give you hope, like they have done for me. I would be lost without them. I wouldn't trade my family for anything in the world.

*"I will be the first one
out of my family
to go to college and
to graduate, too."*

My Parents' Gift

I hope to have a better life than my parents. The life my parents had back then when they were little was hard for them. They lived in Mexico, and they started working at an ever-young age. My mom worked in cooking for the family and also had other jobs picking grapes with her grandmother. My dad had two jobs, as well. First was helping his dad grow crops on the field that they had. Then my dad went with his mother and father to go pick some grapes. That's what they did every day over there in Mexico so they could help their parents pay off the water they used and other stuff as well, like buying food. When they were young, they couldn't go out with any of their friends. There would always be someone telling their parents bad things that they didn't even do, like that they were places that they were not supposed to go but they weren't even there. They always said that they were together, which their parents didn't want them to be for some reason. They would go out and have fun some of the time but not all the time. They went to go ride horses and donkeys for fun (that's what was fun back then) and also play with their friends.

When they decided to cross the border to come to the United States, my mom was seventeen and my dad was nineteen. It was really hard for them to leave their parents behind, and it was hard to walk for a long time with the other groups that were trying to come over as well. Back then, it was a lot easier to cross the border with a lot of people, but now it's difficult to cross without getting caught. When they first got here to the United States, it was different from Mexico, with different stuff that they'd never seen before. The cars were different and also the houses. Also, it was difficult for them to learn the English language. They had to learn English by themselves by hearing other people speak it.

When they got here, they already had some family members living here. They lived with my grandmother. She was the one that help them with getting jobs as well. The jobs that they had were picking cherries from the top of the trees and mostly everyone worked there because they were used to working at those types of jobs over in Mexico. The only thing that they brought over was the clothes that they needed to cross, they left behind almost all of the clothes that they had.

It was very difficult for them to start from ground up. Then couple of months later they had me. They moved to Chicago; that's where I was born. Then, from there, my parents had to move to another place, Omaha, Nebraska. Then, they had to start from ground up—getting jobs and renting a basement in a house that a friend had. It took about three to four years to get enough money to get a house of their own, by renting it first, so from that point in their life, things were better than they were back in Mexico. Then my parents had two more kids—one boy and one girl—so the total of the family would be three boys and two girls.

Watching my parents was hard because they didn't have that much stuff available for us. My mom had one job; it was dry cleaning clothes. And my dad had two jobs to work at cooking food. I didn't get to see them that much every day. When I was getting older, the work my parents had wasn't good enough because of the wages. They didn't have enough money. They inspired me to finish school and get my education to learn something when I go to college. From there, I could open my own business or have a better job than my parents did. That's why they came here—for us to have a better future than they did and have the education that they never had. One time, my parents told me to take advantage of everything that came up for me to have a better future and life, so I wouldn't have to worry about working two jobs as my dad did back then. Also, if I didn't take advantage of everything I had here, what was the point of them coming here if I was going to end up as they did? From that day on, I was thinking a lot about what they had said to me and that they were right. This is what I'm going to tell my brother and sister—to take advantage of everything that can make them have a better future without having bad times or struggling.

When I was ten years old, my older cousin started showing me how to play basketball. It was during the summer, and he was showing me at a park near my house where I live now. It took a year for me to learn how to play it and get better. After that, he stopped teaching me, so I had to learn more about how to play basketball by myself. So I started watching other people at the park and watching games of the NBA to get better at it. My NBA team is the Phoenix Suns, and my favorite player in the NBA is Amare Stoudemire from the New York Knicks. The reason I like this sport is it helps me get some stress out because when I'm playing, I don't focus on the stuff that gets me stressed, like school and the homework at home. It helps me relieve the stress while playing basketball. I have a lot of energy when I start playing basketball. Then, when I get home, I feel better, with no problems or stress; everything is gone. It helps me focus on studying and homework for school.

Everything that I have learned now has been from my parents. From my mom, I learned how to cook things that we eat, like rice, beans, tamales and other things. My mom had gotten the recipes from her grandmother, and she makes them really good. From my dad I have learned a lot, like how to make Chinese food and other stuff that he made up. Also, he has taught me a lot about cars, like how to fix the brakes, disks, gas tank, tires, and transmission, and how to change the oil. Everything that I'm learning now will help me later on in life. So I can show my own kids in the future so they would now how to fix cars, too.

In my free time, I play with my brother and sister. My brother is ten years old, and my little sister is four years old. During the summer, we kick a ball around or just go to the park so they can play around with others. After that, I go out with my cousin and friends to the movies or just go have fun playing video games or sports. Everything that I do, like having fun with friends, my parents didn't have the opportunity to do all because they had to work in the fields with their parents on land that their parents owned. They didn't have everything that I have right now.

My future is going to college to get a good education to learn about fixing cars. I don't know yet what school I want to go to because I haven't been checking any of them. I'm focusing on finishing high school first. So then I can go to college, and then I will have to study hard in all my classes. I will be the first one out of my family to go to college and to graduate, too. The career that I want would be fixing cars because that's what I like to do. After I study more about that career, I could open my own shop to fix cars or just open a shop for my dad to work in. He likes to work on cars; that's what he does almost every afternoon. By doing this career, I would be making a lot of money, and with that, I could get my mom a new house or just fix the house that they are living in now to repay them for all that they did by coming here to give us a better life than they had in Mexico.

I hope to be living here in Omaha because it's a very good place to be, depending on where you live. There are good places to go to and to hang out. Another reason I would want to stay here is to raise my kids here and have a family. My second reason

160

to stay is to be close to family members and friends. If I did decide to move away from Omaha, the other place I would like to live is Miami. There is a beach and warm weather and nice houses to live in, and it's a good place to raise a family as well. Another reason why I would move there is to watch the Miami Heat, which is an NBA team.

I'm very grateful that my parents made sacrifices so that I could have a better life than they did. They gave up a lot by leaving their home and coming to the U.S. It's difficult for them to start over after coming here. They both have taught me so much. I now have opportunities that they could only dream of when they were growing up. I want thank my parents from the bottom of my heart, and I wouldn't trade them for anything in the world.

"I like to picture us
as one of those
big happy families
you see on TV."

A Better Relationship with Dad

When I graduate from high school, I want my dad to be happy and proud of me, knowing that I made it and can be successful in life. And when I walk across the stage and have my diploma in my hand, I want him to have a big smile on his face. I want a big hug from him and to hear him say "I Love You."

What I go through in my life is sometimes difficult. Why, you may ask? It's because what you see is a sweet girl at school, but at home it is different. My life is sometimes difficult because my dad and I don't get along. It makes me so mad and frustrated with him because he acts as if everything is always my fault. It upsets me when my dad and I fight with each other every day because I don't want to yell at him, but he makes me so mad, it just comes right out. I really want me and my dad to get along, but I don't think that it will ever happen because there is too much fighting.

Most days, the words "I love you" are not used in my house. More common is arguing and the word "Whatever!" Yesterday, my sister Mink, my cousin Ashley, and I were just chilling in the living room, watching music videos like always. My dad was in the kitchen next to the living room. I was letting my dogs, Chewy and Travieso, play and run around in the living room while I was watching them. While my dogs were playing, they heard the front door open, and they hurried and ran close to the door as my cousin Joey was coming in. I told him, "Watch out because the dogs are out!" while he was texting on his phone. Joey came in and opened the door slowly, and the dogs hurried and squeezed between his legs out the front door. I went to grab them when Joey saw them trying to run. He grabbed them by the collar, and I took them from him and said, "Can someone please grab Chewy because I got the other one!" Either Mink or Ashley grabbed him, and Mink said, "Joey was laughing," I said, "Why you laughing? 'Cause it ain't funny." He said, "I wasn't laughing." I said, "Sure, whatever," and he replied, "Whatever." Then I told him something that was a little bit mean. When Mink and I were bringing my dogs in, my dad came right in, and he said, "You need to put away your dogs." My sister, Mink, was sticking up for me, and I said, "Well, I told Joey that the dogs were out." My dad yelled, "I don't care. You need to lock your dogs up. I said, "Why? They are always locked up in my room or tied downstairs in the basement when I'm not home." Again, he yelled, "Well, if you don't watch your dogs, I'm going to call the Humane Society." He said, "Watch me." I said, "OK. Whatever." He said the same thing, too, and I laughed, but not because it was funny. It was to show that I know he'll never do it.

For my dad and I to live without arguing would be like a dream come true for me. I like to picture us as one of those one big happy families you see on TV. And yeah, I know that most families aren't like that, but they get along, at least. I wish my dad and I could get along at least for one day, or even one minute. I want us to get along and talk to each other like other families do. And I want him to become one of my close friends.

Occasionally, my dad and I do get along. He sometimes acts silly around me, my sisters, cousin and friends. We even sometimes laugh at each other when one of us does something funny. One day I remember is when my sister, cousin, and I were watching music videos, and my dad started to dance, making us laugh. It was so funny because you know how parents are when they are trying to act cool. Really, it's kind of scary (but in a funny way). That's how it was. And just for a moment, there was no arguing or fighting. It was just hilarious.

I really wish we had more moments like this because I want my dad to show me respect and pride. Yeah, I know that he doesn't show me respect because I don't either, but if he did, then I would, too. I don't want my dad to yell at me when I'm trying to explain my opinion to him. If he didn't yell at me, I wouldn't yell either. I wish he could listen to me when I explain about an issue instead of talking over me. Every time I try to talk to him, he has to say something, but he says it in a bad way, as if everything must be my fault. I don't always think things are my fault, but when he does that, I start to believe it. Sooner or later, I want my dad and I to get along.

It is my time to shine. Soon will I graduate from high school and turn 18, which will make me an adult. I'll be more than just being a silly kid, like some people might think. You are probably like, "Does it make her happy to almost be an adult?" Yes, because soon I can do what I feel like, more than just having to listening to my dad like a kid. Because when you are a kid you have to listen to your family. And I also look forward to making my own decisions instead of having my dad to make my decisions. My hope is not really about that 'cause when I become adult, I want my dad to be on my side. Like if I succeed at something, I want him to be proud of me and say that I can do anything, that there's nothing that can get in my way. And it would make me feel more confidence in myself, you know.

I might not know what's waiting out there for me in my future, but no matter what, I want my dad to always be on my side from the beginning to the end, no matter what differences are between us. I know soon it will be the ending of my high school years. But I want it to be the new beginning chapter in my life in the relationship between my dad and me.

This essay is dedicated in memory of Dominique "Mink" Reyes.

"My children will be strong. They will grow up knowing how to respect and care for everyone, including their father."

Life: Love & Pain

I see myself with the almost perfect family, even though we all know the "perfect family" does not exist. I want to wake up every morning next to the guy I fall in love with and keep falling in love with him more and more every day. I see my kids running into our bedroom, waking us up every morning because they are hungry. My family will be loving and happy. We will have our problems, of course, like every other family, but we will stay together. I don't want my children to go through the pain I went through. Being hurt by your family is the worst pain in the world. It will make you go crazy. When I was going through my pain, I had thoughts of hurting myself. I knew that nothing was more painful than what I was feeling. I was not the same happy person I'd been, and everyone was noticing it. But I didn't like talking about it because it felt as if I were living through it all over again. When I did talk about it, tears would run down my eyes leaving black marks behind. It was just too hard for me, and as a result of my experience, my family's happiness will be the main focus in my life.

It all started when my dad got stabbed in the back by his family. They were doing things behind his back, without his permission. They were trying to give a piece of his land in Mexico to one of my cousins. My dad had that saved piece for his younger brother because his father didn't leave him a piece of land because he had hate towards him. After his mother's death, the youngest one was blamed for it. That made my dad very mad because he felt really betrayed. He tried dealing with it by talking to the people that were involved, but in my eyes, they were just making it worse. Every time he made a phone call to Mexico, we knew without him telling us because he would start to drink. I could see the pain in his eyes, but he never wanted to talk to us about his feelings. He would choose to drink the pain away. That's when he would start picking random fights with my mom every weekend, week after week after week. I was getting really tired of it. I just couldn't take the anger and the sadness every time it happened. All this pain was causing me emotional scars.

One day I was in the kitchen talking with my mom when out of nowhere I thought I heard laughter. I was wrong. It was my younger sister Brenda. She was crying, and my dad was yelling. I wondered what was happening, so I stopped what I was doing and listened. I heard a noise so devastating. It was the sound of my dad hitting my sister. I ran to where they were, but I was too late to stop him. He threw her into the room. I asked what she did wrong, but no answer. So I ran to my sister and hugged her tight. I thought it was to the point where she couldn't breathe. I started crying. I tried to stop my tears, but they kept coming.

These weren't just tears of sadness. They were also filled with hate and guilt. The hate was towards my dad, of course. For some reason, he didn't think that there was anything wrong with hitting my sister. The guilt was because I think that if I would have checked on my sister sooner, she would have never gotten hurt. Still to this day, I feel the same, and every time I think about it tears start running down my cheeks.

I kept seeing my mom and sisters suffer week after week. I just couldn't stand seeing them cry so much. My mom would just take it week after week. I don't know how she did it, but she is a very strong woman. She would cry. How would it not hurt her that all this was going on? But when she cried, she would try to hold it in until she was alone so that no one else would see her because that made her feel weak. My little sisters didn't really know what was going on at first, but they are smart girls. They caught on soon enough. I tried my best at keeping them away from the situation because I didn't want them hearing what was going on, but they could still hear the yelling and see the sadness in all of us. I feel as if I had to be strong in front of my sisters. I didn't want them to see that I was weak until one day when I decided I had been holding it in enough, and I didn't care anymore.

Before this happened, my sister Mari was always a happy and funny person. But after this, she was a more serious person. She was usually the one making me laugh, but now things changed. I tried to make her laugh, and she would just stay serious. Whenever the weekend came and all of this started going on again, it looked to me like she was the one taking it the hardest, and that was weird to me because she was usually the strongest one out of our family. She would never let anything bother her. She would just lock herself in our room and cry and write what she was feeling. Then she would cry herself to sleep. I would sit right next to her, trying to comfort her by hugging her until she fell asleep. One day as she was falling asleep, I found a piece of paper that had her writing on it. I asked her if I could read it, and she said yes. As I read it, my heart dropped, and tears started rolling down my face. This is what she wrote:

Were all those tears and hurt for nothing? Why do I feel so betrayed? Yet every day that passes you act like nothing is wrong. And to me that's just bullshit. In my eyes, I see fear and pain. Wouldn't you rather be heard because I'm here to listen. So many of those tears I guess were worthless because you keep doing what you have been doing before. Think of the family you have created and built. Does that even mean anything to you? I hear you say those words: "but I love you no matter what." Fuck that, love is nothing. Love? If you really loved me, I wouldn't be going through this right now all I ask is why are you doing this? I just think of the drama, and I try to take the pain away differently. Knives, cut myself? Never! Hurt myself for the pain you caused? I wash my tears off slowly with water as I look in the mirror, and I say, if nothing is really happening then why do I feel like my whole world is crashing down on me? Why now? Do I deserve this? So many questions going through my head. I fade into a dark place where I know, no person can hurt me. But is there such a place? Do you love me? If you do, then show me by not hurting me in the worst way possible. I seem to manage getting through day by day with a fake smile on my face, because I want to appear to be strong. But there is only so much I can take. I look away from the mirror because I see your face, and I despise it. The word "hate" never came out while talking about you. But now it comes out like vomit. But I still want you guys to know I actually really do love you. But now I have my middle finger in the air saying fuck you, fuck my life, and fuck the world! Fuck everything!

All this hate I had for my father and all the tears I had been holding back made me explode in a way that I never knew I could. It made me stand up to my dad. That day when my little sister got hit was the day I knew I had enough. I heard my mom and dad in the kitchen arguing about what he had done to my sister. It was getting to the point that I thought he was going to hit her. So I stepped in. I told him that I was getting tired of suffering week after week, and didn't he see how much it affected us? Then he started yelling at me, and I didn't want to stand there and take it, so I tried to walk away but he wanted me there. So he started coming after me, yelling at me. I remember the exact words:

"Get back here."

"No, I don't want to."

"Don't come and see what will happen."

"What you going to do, hit me, too?".

"Why not?!"

I had made it upstairs by the time he said that and he was up in my face. I was wondering if he felt like such a man to put his hands on me, but he just ended up pushing me. After that I felt the most hate toward him because not only did he push me; he tried to push me down the stairs. I knew at that point that I didn't matter to him.

It's as if drinking ruined my family because before all this happened, my dad had stopped drinking. We were just so happy that when all of this started, it killed me inside. But it wasn't little by little; it was all at once and I don't think anyone should take that much pain, especially not all at once. We had been the type of family I always wanted; we did everything together. We would try our best to eat dinner together, but it was hard because before my little sisters got home from school, I was already at work. But on the weekends, there was usually no problem. My favorite thing that we did together was play games like card games or board games. We loved movie nights because that meant family time and all the junk food we wanted!

I'm a kid at heart, so playtime will be a big part of every day with my children when I start a family. I will be my kids' best friend, the person they will come to with confidence whenever they need something or have any problems. It will be like bringing my childhood back to life. My children will be strong. They will grow up knowing how to respect and care for everyone, including their father. My husband will be my prince charming, like in all the fairytales I've read. Unlike my father, he will be there for me through the roller coasters in life. He will love me for what I am and not for what he wants me to be. He will help me accomplish having that perfect family.

"Strength and determination will keep me fighting through life, no matter what it throws my way."

Fighters Keep Fighting

People have to have some kind of push in life, whether it's someone or something that keeps them from quitting that keeps them fighting. I have gone through many things to be where I am now because I kept fighting and never quit. One reason for not quitting is my grandma. She has gone through so many things in her life and still manages to keep going. To see the things she has gone through makes me strong because she made me that way. My sister is another reason why I never quit. She motivates me to succeed and to fulfill my dreams in powerlifting and the UFC.

I love my grandma very much, and to see her today, I am very grateful for her to be in my life and to see me succeed. My grandma made me a fighter because she raised me to never quit and to always believe in myself. Before I was born, she was an alcoholic and while I was growing up, she would always drink. I hated to see her like that, and it broke my heart when it all caught up with her. She went into a coma from all the drinking. I can remember when I was at the hospital and my mother had been told that my grandma would not make it. I cried and cried because I thought I would never see my grandma again. I prayed every night asking God to help my grandma get through this, to wake her up from the coma. A couple of days later, she woke up from her coma, and my prayers were answered. I was so happy that my grandma wasn't going to pass away. After she woke up, I could remember when I went to go see her and she looked at me. My mom asked her who I was, my grandma said, "That's my son." My mom had to tell her that I was her grandson, but I knew that she said that on purpose because she pretty much raised me my entire life.

For a couple of months, my grandma was sober, but then

she ended up drinking again. Not long after that, she drank herself into another coma. I never thought that it would happen again, but it did and I, again, was heartbroken, but two days later she woke up from her coma. This time when she came home with us, she promised me and my mom that she would stay sober. She even started going to AA meetings for help. After about three years of being sober, she needed a liver transplant. I was worried that if she would go through with the procedure she wouldn't make it. My family and I ended up staying at the hospital until the transplant was done. I can still hear the doctors telling us that the transplant was over and that my grandma had made it through. We went up to see her, and I remember my aunt telling her that she is one tough bird. Today, I see my grandma every day, and she has been sober for about ten years. I get to tell her I love her every single day. I don't care what other people see because in my eyes she is a fighter.

Another thing that makes me strong and that makes me a fighter is powerlifting. This sport teaches me to train hard and to not cheat myself because it would make me stronger physically and mentally. I lift everyday because it takes strength and determination to be good at this sport. My sophomore year is when I got introduced to this. My friend told me to join, and I tried it for a while. I ended up liking the atmosphere and it just came naturally to me. Ever since I joined, I have been surprised to see each end result. I would be stronger than I was before in each of my lifts. My confidence went up to an all-time high from sophomore to senior year. In looking at my numbers, I couldn't believe that I was able to lift that much weight. I have come a long way, and I'm not just going to give up now. My goal for powerlifting is to be a state champion for my weight class and to break the school records for my weight division. I have trained very hard. Every day, I push myself past my limits to get where I want to be. I'm a fighter who doesn't know when to quit. I will never quit.

My sister is another reason why I can't give up. She is my motivation to pull through. My sister and I are very close. Our bond is unbreakable. We have been through a lot together, and now we are separated because of some bad choices she made. Every weekend or so my family and I drive up to Geneva to visit her at The Rehabilitation Clinic. Every time I see her, I know that she is fighting to change the way she is because she becomes a more responsible person than she was before. I hate seeing her like this, but if it helps her become a better person, then it's the right thing for her. When I tell her what I want to do in life she doesn't put me down like other people who say things like, "Oh, you won't make it." Instead, she supports me and tells me that it's possible if I believe. She hasn't given up on me, so I can't give up on her. She would do anything to see me succeed.

When I graduate, I want to train for the UFC. The first time I watched it, I became addicted to it. I realized then that I wanted to do that someday. Those fighters got to where they are by being dedicated, and I know that I can dedicate myself to that sport. Most of my life, I have been fighting to get through things and now I want to fight for real. When I watch the fights and I see them coming out to the cage, I picture myself doing that. I picture myself getting into the cage and looking across, toward my opponent, knowing he wants to win just as badly as I do. Two warriors battling each other to see who is better skilled to pull off the win to move them one step closer to a title shot. When I tell my friends that this is what I want to do because I believe that I will be great at this, they just look at me funny and doubt that I can. I pay no attention to what they say because I have a strong will and a strong heart, so I know that I will make it. When I succeed that's when I will know that all my hard work has paid off. I also will know that I will still have to work harder in order to become better so that I can continue in this career.

Strength and determination will keep me fighting through life, no matter what it throws my way. I have people who I'm fighting for and who keep me from quitting. I still have a lot of fight left in me to make this dream come true, and my loved ones will fight for me to see me succeed. Everyone has to fight in life. Whether it's physically, emotionally, or mentally, people still fight. What I learned growing up is that no matter how hard life hits you, it all comes down to how fast you can get back up.

Family: The Influence of Siblings

"My sister was strict with me because of how I behaved in Wyoming, but she also understood why I was doing those things."

Sister's Guidance

Since I was little, I always remember my sister being by my side, either at home or outside playing. She was always there. My dad passed away when I was one, so I never got the chance to know him. My mom went through a really tough time, working a lot to support me, my brother and sister. I didn't get as much quality time as I would have liked. My brother is five years older than me, so he was always out and about with his friends. My sister is three years older. We've stayed close all our lives. She would never leave me; if she went out, I was always welcome to go with her. Up until I was in fifth or sixth grade, we were super close. Then I started hanging out with my friends, and she got a little bit more freedom.

When I was in seventh grade, I came home from school one day and saw a note on my dresser. I thought it was money or a joke. I opened it and started to read. It was from my sister. She had run away, and she told me she loved me and that she was sorry. I just broke down and began to cry. For about an hour, I sat outside my window on the roof, thinking about why and how she did this, thinking about all our times together and how she was gone. I waited until my parents got home and gave my mom the news. She broke into tears. She also found a note on her dresser. I went to my room, gave her a hug and held her, knowing her pain. She and her crying just added more sadness and sorrow to my heart. We called the police, and they showed up in about twenty minutes. We explained the situation, gave them her picture, and they said they would contact us.

The police didn't find out anything. We made it through a rough week, and then my sister called my mom. She had gone to Mexico with her boyfriend. We were angry but happy and relieved that she was ok. It took about a month for us to convince her to come back, and eventually she came. And things were normal for a while.

About a year later, my sister walked into my room, sat down, and said, "If I tell you something, promise you won't tell Mom, even if you're mad." I promised. Then she told me I was going to be an uncle. I was shocked, but at the same time really excited. I promised her I wouldn't tell, and she gave me a hug. After a while of keeping it a secret, she told my mom. My mom was mad but got over it quickly. After we all got used to the idea, we were really anxious to meet our new family member.

At that time, my sister and her boyfriend weren't exactly happy all the time. They had moved in with us, and it seemed all they did was argue. After nine months of this, the day finally came. I was in my room, and I heard my mom screaming for me to get my shoes on because we were leaving for the hospital. I was confused and kind of scared. We all rushed in the car and took off to the hospital. We got there, and they put my sister on those rolling beds and took her to a room. My brother-in-law and I waited outside the room for about an hour. Then the doctors came out and said, "You may go in." We ran in there and saw everyone surrounding the bed. My sister was holding the cutest baby girl I'd ever seen. My parents were crying and other people were, too. I held my new niece and just watched her sleep. She looked like a toy doll, so small and fragile.

Soon after my niece was born, my stepdad was offered a better job in Wyoming. I was really upset at the news. Things were really good for me at that point in my life. All this meant a new city, new friends, new house, new life. Problem was, I liked my old one. Wyoming wasn't the best place ever. When we got there, first thing I noticed is you could see the borders of where the town started and ended. In the morning, we went to go look around town. It was the smallest town I had ever seen. It only had one high school, one middle school, and one elementary. They didn't even have a WalMart. But eventually, we all learned to adjust.

After my sister and her boyfriend settled down, they got their own apartment in Omaha, they bought a truck, and they were doing pretty good. It stayed like this for about a year or so. Everything was going great, but I could sense stress in my sister. She always looked tired; it seemed like the parent job was getting to her. Things got pretty rocky, and her and her boyfriend split up. It seemed weird to me why this happened if she was living good. Then, the news came about a week later—my sister was pregnant again. I was really excited because I wanted a boy this time.

My sister wasn't sad but was not super-excited. She wasn't financially or mentally ready to go through pregnancy again, but what are you going to do? So, again, it was another nine months of my sister getting fat and eating weird foods. This time, it went a lot quicker than the last time. It's like I knew what to expect, so it took the excitement away. So nine months later, my other niece was born.

After not seeing my nieces for some months, we finally came back from Wyoming for vacation. I was still over at my sister's house a lot and still was close with her. Most weekends and weekdays, I was over at my sister's house, playing with my nieces or hanging out with friends around the neighborhood. Around this time, I turned 15, and I kind of started doing my own thing. I started going out a lot to parties, movies, and out to a lot of places. I was at the age where you just want to have fun. Everything was great. I was home with my family, surrounded by friends. Things were all in place. But I could never forget that this was just a vacation. Soon I would be back in Wyoming. On the way to Wyoming, all I could think about was all the things I was gonna miss out on in Omaha. The ten-hour trip seemed like twenty. When we got there, I went to my room, turned off the light and just sat in the silence, thinking long and hard about my life and how it would change me living in this small town. School was ok. I knew some people from last time I was there. I started hanging out with people you wouldn't exactly want to be your kid's role model. But I just blamed everyone else for everything. I started to rebel against my parents and getting into trouble. I used to think that it was so boring, that trouble was the only fun. I got in fights in school, started smoking a lot of pot, and really steering out of control. My mom told my sister, and my sister convinced her it was better for me to move back. No need to say, I agreed.

So I moved back to Omaha, and I was happier than ever. I was so happy to be back with my sister and her family. My sister was strict with me because of how I behaved in Wyoming, but she also understood why I was doing those things. Omaha felt so great; it just felt like home. I was back to my old self and found out my parents were coming back.

So, that kind of brings us up to speed to today. I'm back in school, trying to graduate, and my sister and nieces are just a call away. My sister recently moved into a new apartment, and my nieces are now two and three, still the cutest things ever. My sister is my inspiration for hope because despite all the bumps along the road, she never gave up for her, me, and most importantly my nieces—the ones I love most.

"I want her to know the importance of working hard and staying in school."

A Day With Me

I start my story with the birth of my youngest sister, Nichole Perez, the most incredible thing to happen to me to date. I never thought I could care for someone as much as I do her. At that time in my life, I was an apathetic preteen who didn't want to care about a thing in my life, until she came in. I love that baby with all my being. She helped me realize how much life is worth and that family is always more important than anything material, friends or work. She helped the family by being the life of the house while our family was going through rough times. No matter how hard things got, you couldn't help but hold her and feel overwhelmed with joy and that even when it seemed like life was bad, there was something so innocent and beautiful to keep you going and trying your hardest.

Things took a turn for the worse when my mother was diagnosed with cancer in her collarbone. Her diagnosis added a lot more stress on the family. Not long after, my father suffered an injury at work and was wrongfully let go. Without his income, bills started stacking up, and stress and pressure increased on our family. As soon as my dad was capable of working, he got a job at Greater Omaha where the pay was poor and the hours were long. Furthermore, my mother was very ill and always in bed.

Things looked like they couldn't get any worse, and as it turned out we were one payment away from losing our house. Eventually, my mom fully recuperated from her illness, and my dad left town for a supposedly better job. I say supposedly because the pay was much better, but the work was an immense stress on him. My mother also applied for a job there, and as a result, the whole family moved to Iowa. I didn't want want to go; my friends, my work, my life was here in Omaha. I wanted to be with my family, but how would I get volunteer work done plus the clubs, sports and activities that would help me get into college? It would all be so hard not knowing anyone. And it being my last year in school, and I would have had to graduate in a dinky little town with not a familiar face in my graduating class?? I decided to stay here in Omaha, and with my parents help I have done so. My parents help me out here and there. "Hon, do you need money, milk, groceries?" they ask. I say, "No, I'm good." I provide all that I can for myself because I don't want them worrying about me. They have enough on their plate, and I will not be another burden.

I recently bought a car. It seems like a stupid decision, but I needed something for the winter. I hate waking up in the morning and having to walk to school in subzero temperatures. Plus, I am sick and tired of asking for a ride everywhere I need to go, and I know friends and family are fed up with it as well. No matter how much they say it's cool, I know it's not.

I see my parents once a week, sometimes not at all. I do miss them. I miss my entire family, and I wish I could see them a lot more. My mother trusts me and trusts that I will not take advantage of my freedom. Doing so would break my mother's heart. I currently work every day that I can in order to pay off a car that I just bought. I am living off the change in my dresser and have even had to resort to asking friends for money. My best friend who has helped me through so much recently is Samahara. I met on her first day at work, and I have been stuck on her since. I tell her everything, and she tells me everything. She lent me $80 and did not set a deadline. "Whenever you can," she said, not giving it a second thought when she handed me the money. I help her through her struggles just as she helps me through mine. I love her dearly and consider her a big part of my life.

I have been talking to my younger sister. She turns 17 in April. She is having trouble adjusting to the new town. My sister is an outstandingly beautiful young woman. Not only that, but she also has great morals and respects herself. She does not let anyone disrespect her, which creates a lot of problems at her new school. She has been in a fight already—winning, of course—but creating concern for my parents. I love my sister and cannot stand to see her going through so much. I am fighting for my parents to let her come stay with me, failing so far, but I am willing to sacrifice a lot more in order to have her here with me.

What I see happening in the future is the commencement of a new life. I want to go to school and work with the help of my family. Even though they help me now, it's not the same as having them here in Omaha. Once my parents are out of debt and my dad completes his GED, it will increase our opportunity for a better life. He will have the money to provide my younger sisters with all the things that he could not provide for me or my other sister. At the same time, I hope my baby sister does not become spoiled. I want her to grow up knowing our struggle and to embrace it and for her to try harder than me and to be successful. Even from a young age, I want her to know the importance of working hard and staying in school. I want to go to the University of Nebraska for a bachelor's degree, but it seems like I will have to start off at a community college first and transfer later to a four-year school. Of course, I do not mind that I will have to work hard in order to get a scholarship that will cover my tuition because frankly, I do not believe I will be able to afford college without financing nor do I believe in digging myself into debt. I plan on working hard to keep myself in school and away from the wrong path. My sister keeps me going because she is so innocent, and no matter what I do, she will always be there for me.

"When I thought about hope and where I find it, it made me think of all the good times I had when I was little because I associate happiness with hope."

Occam's Razor of Hope

I found my hope through family because of how close my family is. We spend a lot of time together, especially during the holidays and vacation. I think that hope is easily found in family because family is important to everyone, especially to younger children.

As children, my older brother and my two cousins played outside every day. We would ride our bikes around the neighborhood and through Spring Lake Park. The neighborhood we lived in (and still live in) is in the city yet somewhat secluded and surrounded by a forest-like area filled with trees that would easily be more than a hundred years old. Riding through the terrain was fun because it's a different experience than riding on a cement road. I would sometimes pretend that we were riding a dirt bike, jumping off ramps.

I always hung out with my older brother, Josue, and my two cousins, Fernando and Yesenia. My brother was not that much older than I am (only 18 months), but he was stronger, taller, and wiser than I was. Now I am taller than him and everyone else in my family. He is still somewhat smarter, but I'm unsure who is stronger. Fernando, my cousin, is older than Josue, but wiser as well as stronger. He used to be tall, but as I mentioned before, I am taller than everyone in my family. Fernando is also artistic. He's never taken an art class, so I assume he was born with that talent. His drawings are amazing; they have such detail to them that they look like a picture taken with a camera. Yesenia is Fernando's little sister and the same age as my brother Josue. She is also artistic and skilled in sewing; she has fixed some of my shirts before and made a small bag in the shape of a bear with buttons for eyes and the zipper for its mouth.

Every summer, we would go to Mexico for a couple of

weeks. We would travel by car ...well, truck. The drive from Omaha to Reynosa was about twenty-two hours. During the trip, I would stay up, staring out the window, looking at houses, farms, barns, and the terrain of the land. Before we left, we would stop by Burger King and pick up some Whoppers to go. When we would stop for gas, I would go in the store and buy a bag of chips and a drink, mostly Gatorade. When we finally arrived in Mexico, it would be really early in the morning, like around four o'clock.

Being in Mexico is a change of scenery (mostly temperature-wise). Houses made of concrete, dirt roads around neighborhoods, a small convenience store and restaurants within walking distance. There are more places to visit, like traveling amusement parks, a cave with rocks that still have fossils embedded in them, a beautiful waterfall that resembles a horse's tail, and a big open area known as El Centro, where you can buy the many things people have to offer, like soccer t-shirts, wallets and Mexican candy, and try the delicious food made by hand, like churros. Sometimes, we would go to a small town called San Benito. In the town, people own some of the land, and I learned that my Grandfather owns a large portion. I like it there because it's quiet and at night the stars are out and easily visible. In Omaha, just the moon and a few bright stars are visible, which I kind of hate because I like looking up at the stars every once in a while. There are times when people just want to look up at the sky and stare at the stars.

I know I'm supposed to be writing about hope and not my childhood, but when I thought about hope and where I find it, it made me think of all the good times I had when I was little because I associate happiness with hope. When my father was little, he had a rough childhood and yet found enjoyment in going to school. I guess going to school gave him hope to live a better life, not just for him but for his future family as well. That is what he also wants for his kids (me and my siblings) to do as well. I guess my point is that hope can be found anywhere, even in the smallest and simplest of places.

Family: Children & Future Family

*"As I move forward,
I can honestly say that
I made it, and I can
smile big to the people
that doubted me."*

Growing Up Fast

When I think about hope, I think about how I'm going to make it in life. What kind of person will I be? I think about how my son will be in the future. I know that I want to succeed and have my son have everything possible that I never had. People doubt that I'm going to make it. But I know that I am going to make it. Nothing will stop me from success. And I know my son will have it better than what I had growing up.

Growing up for me was not cool or great. It was horrifying! I saw my mom and brother get beat by my drunken father. I couldn't do anything. He was so much stronger than me. All I did was cry in the corner and watch every hit and every punch my mom or brother got. And hearing them cry made it worse. I was so scared that I didn't know who to tell. So I just kept quiet. I didn't understand why this was happening to our family. I went through this for about nine years of my life. My dad never touched me because I guess he loved me more than my mom or brother. I was so lost about what that meant, but I knew that he wouldn't touch me. When those nine years ended, my father left and never came back. I got so angry inside. I thought it was my fault that he left. I would cry all the time. I never wanted our family to break apart, but it did. After my father left, I didn't care about life anymore. Yeah, I was too young to know what life was really about. But the point was I didn't want to listen no more to my mom. I wanted to just run off on the street, to not let anybody tell me what to do anymore. Eventually, I got caught. I got put in the court system. I was taken away from my mom's home and put in a foster home and also in other places. I didn't take nothing serious until I found out I was pregnant. I was only 16. That's when I got a message through my head that I needed to change my ways and fast.

My whole life changed after I got pregnant. I had someone else's life in my hand. I knew that they were going to depend on me now. There wasn't any time to jack around or get in trouble. It was time to get serious! I knew it was already going to be hard because the baby daddy was not going to be there. But with the support of my family, I'm going to make it! All the help I received while I was pregnant was very helpful. It made me realize that so many people cared for me. I want the best for my son, Giovanni. And as a single mom, it's hard, but I'm still trying to maintain. And yeah, it took me getting to the point where I had to get pregnant to realize that my life isn't no joke no more. But I know it was a gift from God that all this happened.

Now that I'm growing up and my son is growing each day, I try to do my hardest to finish school. I don't know what I want to be yet. All I know is that I want a higher education to get a good job. I'm taking my life as serious as I can because I barely just got placed back in my mom's home. So everything I do, the workers will still watch. I feel I still get watched all the time. It makes me feel like I'm not trusted enough for my workers to get off my back. When I don't feel trusted enough, I feel like I'm doing something wrong or that they just try to get me to feel like I'm a bad person. I don't let this bother me, so I move on and parent my son and work hard in school.

Yeah, parenting is so hard, but now that I have a supportive boyfriend, he is going to start helping me. I thank him a lot because at times I want to give up and he brings me back up. My future with him is so amazing. I want a baby girl by him. Her name would be Elena. He would be a good dad to her and also to my son. I want us to move forward and have good jobs that will help us money-wise. I imagine a beautiful brown-tannish house with lots of windows and flowers. The inside would smell like home sweet home. And yeah, of course we're not going to have a perfect life and some people may think I'm crazy, but I want to move up and not depend on my mom to pay for me to live in the house. I want to move out on my own and be an independent woman. I want to help myself and my son. As I move forward, I can honestly say that I made it, and I can smile big to the people that doubted me. I know that I have reached my highest and nothing will stop me from succeeding.

"It was a life-changing experience, and now I'm going somewhere in my life."

And Baby Makes Me

Once upon a time, there was this girl who did not think of college or even of going anywhere after high school. She also did not think of a career or what she would want to do. She lived in what you call "The Now." She didn't care what happened in her past or what was going to happen in her future, let alone did she know that her past was going to better her life or that it was what was going to make her future. Then, on the day her son was born, she realized what she wanted and that life was real and that she could no longer live only in "The Now."

Now it may come to no surprise that I am that girl who had no dreams or hope. I grew up the child of two very different people. My mother is a short, green-eyed, strawberry blonde with endless energy who never forgets to hug, kiss, play around and love her four children. She is my most favorite person in the world, and behind her oval glasses is a woman who has always made my brothers and me her highest priority. She is open and understanding about everything and anything. My relationship with her is great. I mean, everyone has their days and those fights where you say stuff that you don't mean and would have never said if you were not mad. So besides those times, which are very rare, me and my mom get along great.

My father, on the other hand, is as dark as my mother is light. He is a short, dark-eyed, dark-haired man who I love and used to go everywhere with. I was attached to his hip. He was my most favorite thing at that time. He is my dad, and I love him. Our relationship now is very different. I love him so much, but still, he's not there. I try to be around him and talk to him all the time, and still, I can try so hard and the only time it seems he's there for me is when he's in jail or prison. At those times, I feel like I just want to hate him and be able to say *forget him* because when he gets out, he's going to stop being there or talking to me. But NO, I don't do that. I feel sorry for him and so I go see him every chance I can and write him everyday and put money on his books. I'm the only one there for him, and still it seems as though he still doesn't care after he gets out. And I sit there and tell myself over and over, "Stop. Don't care what happens to him because you're just going to get hurt again." But even though I know in the end what I'll feel like and what's going to happen, I still care about him.

My dad never helped my mom when they broke up; he just went on with his life, not helping her. She raised me and my brother by herself. She had a job, she paid the bills, bought school clothes, etc. My dad? He has done none of that. Even now, he does nothing. I know how my dad treated my mom and the way he made her feel, but when my mom got remarried, I kind of felt as if I hated her. All I wanted was to have my parents together even though he hurt her. When she got remarried to my stepdad, I did not like him at all. He was not my dad, and he was not going to tell me what to do. This guy was no one to me; he was just my mom's husband. Now we are fine and have a better relationship. It took a long time to get there, but I finally came around. Although me and my stepdad were getting along, my dad and I were not. When I told my mom I was pregnant, she said I had to tell my dad. I didn't want to. So she called and told him, and he said, "Let me talk to her." I got on the phone with him, and I was sitting on the couch in my pajamas, and of course I was crying. Then he told me, "You're stupid. What the hell were you thinking?" And I got mad because how does he have the right to be mad at me and say that to me when he was never around? So I got mad and threw the phone, and my mom asked, "What happened?" So I told her, and she was mad. She got on the phone with him, and they got into it because of what he said to me. My mom said so many things to him that I would say here, but they're not good at all.

That kind of leads into letting you know that, yes, I had a little baby boy. I got pregnant at 16, and it was close to the end of my sophomore year. At first, I did not tell anyone—not even my mom—that I was pregnant. It was hard being pregnant and not telling anyone but my boyfriend because it always seemed as if every person I saw was staring and saying stuff, but I tried not letting it bother me. People at school stared and thought what they wanted and assumed whatever they wanted. Soon enough, I told everyone and my mom that I was six months pregnant, and then it was like a huge relief was off my shoulders. Then everything was fine, and besides, I was pregnant all through the summer. (Boy, does that make you hotter.)

I remember the day I had my son like it was yesterday. That night, I was at my boyfriend's house. We had a cookout. It was close to midnight and my stomach was hurting, so my mom came and got me. I just thought I was sick because I ate so much. So when I got home, I ended up getting sick and threw up. Then I told my mom, "I'm going to take a shower and go lay down." She said, "All right, if you need anything, let me know." So I took a shower, got dressed, laid down and started watching TV. Then I was getting tired. It was about 2:40 a.m. I turned the TV off and turned over to go to sleep. Then, I felt as if I had to go to the restroom. I stood up a heard a little pop sound and water started running down my leg. I ran upstairs to my mom, who had just taken some medicine to go to sleep. I said, "Mom, I think my water broke because I know I am not peeing." So she told my brothers and called my grandma and my stepdad, so he came home and drove us to the hospital while my mom left to get my boyfriend.

When I was in labor and in pain, the nurses could have not

been more caring. They seemed as if they were not just there because it was their job but because they wanted to be. During the whole thing, the nurse I had was great. She even came in at one point and sat with my family and talked like she knew us forever, which to me was really nice. She came and checked on me about every five or six minutes, and she even took pictures with me. She said she had a double shift that night and that they were going to assign me another nurse for the night but she said, "No, I want to stay her nurse." So I was in labor for 28 hours, and she was the one to give me the bad news that I had only dilated to seven centimeters. So the doctor decided to do a C-section, and at 4:01 a.m., I welcomed my baby son, Alex Dillon Koch, into the world (at 7 lb 4 oz and 21 inches long). He is my pride and joy. The whole time I was at the hospital, the nurses were great, especially Nurse Jones, and that experience is what made me want even more to become an RN and work in labor and delivery.

A career in nursing is very important to me. It's so important to me because I believe it will better my life in so many ways. I want a career because I believe that a career is better than a regular job that anyone can go get, like working at a store or a pizza place. I mean, that is a job, and I am not saying working at one of those places is bad or that it makes you a lower person, so don't get me wrong. But to me, having a career is more stable, which is what I want, because then I won't have to go day-to-day wondering if my paycheck will be enough this week to pay the bills or to get food for my son. That then leads to another reason I want a career: to support my son and make sure I have what he needs and the money to get it when he needs it. Also, I want to be able to get him more than just what he needs. I want to get him what he wants. Like when we go in a store and he wants a little three dollar toy, I want to be able to say, "Ok, throw it in the cart." I don't want to have to say, "No, I don't have the money," when it's only three dollars. Then, finally, I just want to have the comfort of knowing everything will be ok and that I don't have to stress so hard and work my butt off for nothing.

Now, after hearing all this, everyone probably wonders how I am going to get there. How am I going to get what I want and make it happen? It will be hard, especially with my son. But that is ok. It may be hard because of my son, but on the other hand, he's also the one who motivates me and makes me work hard. Now the way I'm going to meet my goals is through lots of support, because support from my family is very important to me. I also am going to work hard, making sure that all work is done and turned in on time, and I will work to my fullest potential. Another way I will get to what I want is through grants and filling out the form for Federal Student Aid. I know that is a long process and a hard one, but if that is the only way to get to college and get started, then that's what I will do. The final thing that I need to do is lots of college visits, find out what the colleges offer, and what scholarships they may offer to a good student who is also a mother.

I started out not wanting to go anywhere after high school or even thinking of a career. I have been through a lot, and that's ok because I'm not complaining. I also would never go back and change anything, like not having my son or my relationship with my parents. Lots of people say having a baby young is not good, that you are not going to make it and, yes, I have seen lots of young parents not make it. But in my case, it was a life-changing experience, and now I'm going somewhere in my life. This does not mean I would ever tell someone to ever go get pregnant to better their life, but it certainly has changed mine for the best.

"Faith takes faith, and hope requires action."

To Marriage, Then Motherhood

Women nowadays lead two lives. One is career-driven; this is when most women put forth the most effort and skill to accomplish a never-ending task. The other and the subtler of the two, is raising a family solely by staying home (cooking, cleaning, writing, or even taking online college courses). My future is homemaking. I chose this; it is *not* forced upon me in any way. I was raised to be home bodied and skilled in its requirements. Therefore, my hope is that I journey into motherly maturity and forget nothing of myself along the way.

I was one of those children who grew up with two parents. By the time my younger brother was born, they were divorced. I was five years old then, and I can't really explain how it affected me because I am still trying to figure that out. The only truth that came out of the divorce was that I will never have a typical father, one who would talk to me every day or understand my feelings. After the divorce, he just moved into an apartment and thought the only way we could spend time together was on the days we were required to by law. So I was raised by my mother, which is and was fine for me but wasn't for my brother. But before our parents divorced, when I was two years old, my mother was still in her twenties and always wanted to be outside and on the move. We used to do productive things like go to a park and take walks in the afternoon followed by a nap. I remember playing in a ball pit at Westroads Mall (it was like diving into a solid rainbow) and watching *Mulan* at AMC. But then, when I turned two, she had to get a job to support our family's income. She was no longer able to be a stay-at-home mom. During this time, I stayed home with my dad (he worked evenings and she all day). Those days are blurry to me now. I never watched too much television before my mother got a job, but now I was watching Barney and Sesame Street at every hour of the morning.

Even though I spent the first two years of my existence on this planet always outdoors and shopping with my mother, I never have sporadic urges to go somewhere and/or *buy* something. I feel that my mother raised me well this way with values and morals. I was home bodied, and I liked to go outside once in a while. Even today, I stay home most of the weekend. If we do go out, it is to buy groceries or sit at Barnes & Noble.

One time at B&N, I saw *What to Expect When You're Expecting* and laughed. I literally burst out in bubbles of giggles. When my mom asked what made me laugh so spontaneously, I replied by showing her the book. She looked at me with a quizzical expression as if she was thinking that I was thinking about expecting.

She gave me some pretty good insight too: "You don't need a book to know what to do. It just comes, like when you discover you really love a plot in a novel; you'll know what to do then. It's like a light bulb, an *ah-ha!* moment. And if not, I'll always be there."

I laughed again and agreed but secretly knew I'd read that book one day. Then I asked, "What if I want to put headsets on my belly? Will that be okay?"

"Yes, yes, that works, too," she said with a smile.

My mother's influence greatly impacts my future. I am of the age now where I can bake my cake and eat it too, sans regrets. I am encouraged to make major decisions; I am in control of my life though still under my mother's guidance. I was raised the "old-fashioned" way—to have good values and morals. And even amidst a career-women-empowered society, I choose to be empowering in the home.

Ideally, my own home in the near future would be spick and span. I hope it would have an all-weather porch in the front or back of the house, so that I can read in the sheltered environment I was raised in. I don't want a big house, just a house with big bedrooms and *several* bathrooms. (I grew up in a house with one bathroom for twelve years.)

Before my ideal home will come my ideal marriage to a partner who can provide a home and car, is able to want and rear children, and has a stable job that offers health insurance for the both of us. My model husband would be a man who is more spiritually intelligent than I am and book-smart; he should be able and willing to express his true self with me in *all* situations. And, typically, he has to be honest and communicative, because without those two traits, there is no relationship and thus no moving forward. I don't need someone to always make me laugh, but what I do need is a man who won't make me drive and who is appreciative of the food I prepare or the way I make the bed—the simple things. I hope to find a man like this so if we were to have four boys and stay together until death, they won't be like my brother and have to grow up without a father. I would never wish that pain on anyone. A boy needs his father as much as a girl needs her mother and they both need both parents. Enough said.

I believe in fate, to let hope implement action. Therefore, whomever I am meant to be with will come along. I have never dated before, so this doesn't mean I can just wait around for it happen. I need to travel to find my future destination. Right now, I'm set on the west coast, partially because there isn't much snow or ice, and there are close-knit spiritual communities. I've already taken trips to Colorado and Arizona, but I'm focusing more on Washington or Oregon.

Washington has been on my family's mind for seventeen years. When my mother and father were almost parents in 1994, they took a trip up to Seattle. My father was scouting the country for job openings in the travel field, and Seattle was an option. They liked it there with the rainy weather and mountainous terrain. They said it would have been a great place to raise a child. My parents, however, chose Omaha, Nebraska, because it was a small city full of family qualities. I always wonder about Washington, if we'd have a two-story house, if I'd go to an academy or have more siblings. I'm positive I'd have still turned out the same with the old-fashioned mentality and "career" choice.

Now, seventeen years later, my mother, brother, and I are ready to move away; we are ready to make the best decision of our lives. In Omaha, we have everything a middle-class family can afford: more than one car, a house, a parent with a stable job. What we don't have is a spiritual community. In my opinion, the faithful are keeping to themselves (almost reclusively), and the faithless are loose on the streets. Of course there will be these two types of people anywhere we go, but hopefully, there will be more of the faithful. The things that we have now are simply so, just *things*. Without spirituality, it's like we have nothing. We really don't have any connection to this life without the golden thread—faith. That's how I believe, anyway. I can't simply see faith; I must implement it into my life.

So comes the nitty-gritty of traveling and moving. *That* is my immediate future. To get there, so many people in my life have either pushed me forward or pulled me back. What others think I should be is often how they want to be, but they are also pulled back from their hopes and dreams. My father, for example, always wanted me to get an education and become a teacher. I'm fulfilling part of his "request;" I can teach *my* children at *home*. A lot of my friends believe my intelligence will simply be abducted from my mind if I am at home all day. Well, then I shall be on a social schedule. Preferably it will work as so (before children, with a working husband): I would make breakfast, clean the house top to bottom, maybe take a nap, make lunch (husband comes home on break), go someplace with my mother/miscellaneous outing (i.e. book club, getting my librarian certificate, or taking courses in massage), wait for husband to get home, we go out or stay in. What is so reclusive about that? Plus, I will *always, always, always* tell my husband where I am, even if I am visiting a neighbor or taking a stroll, whether he expects that of me or not. Communication, as mentioned earlier, is imbedded into my conscience.

Furthermore, I am, in a way, rebelling against modern society's standards. Not only do I feel strong in my decision, I feel a bit … *good* for defying modern mores. I want nothing more than this aspiration to lead my life. I am who I am. No one can change that because God has written that path for me. Faith takes faith, and hope requires action.

Callings & Work

"Growing up broke is never fun, but I believe it has made me a better person, and I can really respect a hard-working man."

Life Under the Hood

As a kid growing up, I only have had one parent: my mom. So the money has never really been there, and we have always lived paycheck to paycheck. My mom works as a cleaning lady, and it doesn't pay a whole lot of money. It seemed that whenever we were really broke, the cars we owned always broke down. So eventually, my brother and I decided to learn how to work on cars. The first car I ever worked on was a firecracker-red '96 Ford Escort. I remember always going on camping trips to Fremont and Louisville, Nebraska, in it. I think I was about seven years old and my brother is six years older than me, so we were very young when we began. My brother and I have always had a talent for handyman-type work, and I believe we take after our father.

Since I've started working on cars, it's almost come to me naturally, and I've enjoyed every bit of it. Even when I'm broke and something breaks down on my vehicle, I'm always happy to fix it. When my brother and I work on cars, we spend time together that we don't usually get, and we really get to know each other even more. Otherwise, we would never really spend a whole lot of time with each other because he works most of the time. I feel more normal working on cars with my brother and friends than in anything else we do together. When I work on cars, it seems to clear my mind and keep me focused. It's working on a car that reminds me of fishing or outdoors; it seems to refresh me and keep me going. When I say I'm going to work on cars to other people after I get off work, they think I'm crazy. I always hear, "You work too much," but in reality, I can't wait to pop the hood and get to work.

My brother's name is Matt. He is big—about 320 pounds, 6' 5", and very smart. Growing up, he always liked Chevys and really sparked my love for them. I would have to say the 1969 Chevy Nova SS 396 (the L78 package) is my favorite ride. Since the day I laid eyes on that car when it was sitting in my friend Mike's grandfather's garage, I couldn't get out of my mind how badly I wanted to buy and restore that car. I could drive that car forever, and I believe I will always drive an older vehicle just like the Nova for the rest of my life. I'd rather drive an older vehicle because maintaining it is simple, parts are cheap, and I like the classic look.

Since I began working on cars, I've always wanted to be a master mechanic. I've had the same goal all through school. I'm hoping to take my skills and make them better by going to an automotive school. A big part of being a mechanic today is knowing electrical systems, for instance, diagnosing ohms. When you have the knowledge and the skill to do something, you have the ability to be great at it. When I finish with the automotive schooling, I plan to try and open my own shop. My brother, friends and I have been talking for a couple of years about all of us opening a shop. I believe the skill is there, but the money and time are lacking. But I know that once I get into something like auto repair and become successful, there will be no stopping me.

It has been a long journey to get to this point, hard-fought to say the least. I am grateful for all my family has done for me even through the tough times, but that is making me work harder so I can give my family in the future the life I never had. Growing up broke is never fun, but I believe it has made me a better person, and I can really respect a hard-working man.

"I get motivated when someone tells me something good or when someone tells me bad things, I want to prove them wrong."

My Struggle

I remember the first time my dad cut my hair. I didn't like what he had done. It just didn't look right. I was really upset. I thought to myself that I could cut my hair a little better than my dad. So I thought I would give it a shot. So, one day I was hanging with one of my homeboys, and he asked me if I could cut his hair. I told him I could, so he described to me what he would like his hair to look like. I pictured it and what I could do. I starting cutting his hair, and when I was done it looked real good. That was the day I told myself I could be a barber, and I started picturing what I could do when I got older.

I know what I need to do to be a barber. First I need 11 more credits to graduate from high school. That's a little harder than it sounds. Finishing every credit is made much harder because I struggle maintaining focus and being motivated. Then, I have to go to barber college; I already have the application. But I am kind of lazy and sometimes don't feel like doing what I want to do. I couldn't tell you why, but I think it would have something to do with my motivation. I get frustrated when I don't have help on my work when it's needed. Some things are really confusing, like reading a book and understanding after I read. My reading skills are not that good. When I'm reading, I tend to mess up, and then I get mad and I give up on it.

I'm not that motivated when it comes to school. It also is hard to stay focused on my schoolwork because I get angry when things are not clicking in my head. Sometimes, when I am reading, I know what they are saying, but I don't know what they mean. But I try to understand at first and then if I don't get it, my feelings for reading start falling downhill.

Not getting enough sleep is another reason I'm lazy. I get tired and my body feels weak sometimes. I am too young to feel weak when I am tired. That's when I get really lazy so my excitement is not very high for doing schoolwork.

I'm trying to change my bad habits, but sometimes I get that feeling again when I just don't care and don't want to do anything. I feel this sometimes because my frustration gets me down. It's making feel like I am nothing and won't be anything. I tell myself that I don't want a good education, but I know that I want my education. To get my education, making the right choices would be the best problem to solve. Hanging around the right people could influence my motivation to reach my goals. Getting lots of sleep so I can be energized. Seeing my mom also motivates me a lot in school; she helps me be confident about anything I'm doing. I try to see her about once a week; it has been that way since we were evicted. The last time I saw her, she braided my hair. We hung out for about an hour. She asked me how I'm doing and how I'm doing in school. I tell her that I'm trying to keep my grades up, but it's hard. Mom gives me energy; she always told me things I wanted to hear. She tries to make me feel good inside when I am down or frustrated. She says things like to keep trying and hold my head high and prove to myself that I can graduate. She likes to use her past to influence me to do better.

I feel motivated when I know what I am doing on some homework or something that I am interested in. I get motivated when someone tells me something good or when someone tells me bad things, I want to prove them wrong. I don't accept when others talk about me and what I do. So I get upset and begin to feel like I've got to do something really spectacular to prove that I'm better than they think I am.

The last time I was motivated was when I was writing this story about what I want in my life and my problems. Writing this story helped me get out some of my problems because I have lots of problems in my life. So does everyone else in this life that we live, but my issue is that I never try to fix my problems. I keep them inside of me, and they drive me crazy at times. But I am beginning to change that around. If I need to say something, I may speak to myself or share it with my little sister because she somewhat understands me. But I mainly speak to myself because I can just lay it out and forget about everything I said.

When I am not motivated, I don't want to do anything. I'd rather sit at home and watch a TV show or play video games. I don't like doing schoolwork because school doesn't interest me enough to do it. To me, schoolwork is boring, but what I want to be takes a high school diploma or GED. So I'm forced to do my homework. Schoolwork could be more interesting if it was hands-on, like working on a car or learning stuff about how the world works or how things are made in the world.

"My first step on my journey was changing my attitude, my ways and my thinking process."

What Do You See When You Look in the Mirror?

What do you see when you look into the mirror? Are you just looking to see if your hair looks nice, or if your clothes fit right? When I look into the mirror, I see more. I see my future, my goals, and what I'm setting out to be. Yes, I might check my hair and look at my shirt, but I'm looking at a message to myself. On my mirror, I write messages to prepare me for my future to remind myself what I am working for, why I push myself everyday! Owning my business is in my future, teaching a class of juniors and seniors in high school is also what I see, with a possibility of working in a private practice. Writing on the mirror is a start, but acting on it is also important. Every day, I wake up, I look and remind myself what to look forward to. The mirror I look into motivates me to be a better me.

I haven't always used this mirror to look into my future. Before, when I looked in the mirror, I would just glance and think to myself, "I am an unhappy girl who pretends to be happy." The girl I saw in the mirror was a lie and was something I was tired of looking at. So I realized I have to change before I make a mistake that can dictate my future. Change doesn't come easy, I had to go through trials and tribulations, the high and the low, to get to where I am. You couldn't tell me freshman year that I would make it to senior year and have senior credits. You couldn't tell me that I was going to graduate on time. I made a lot of mistakes in my past—bad grades, staying out late, breaking rules, running away, all of the above. With those negative mistakes, there also came positive growth. I opened up my eyes and realized if I continued to go down that path, that my future wasn't guaranteed, so I started to change. I changed my attitude and how I looked at things, started being happy within myself and actually started working toward a successful future. I wanted to be the girl who knew that she was going to graduate on time. My first step on my journey was changing my attitude, my ways and my thinking process.

I started staying home more, working a lot just to keep myself off streets and calm myself down from always wanting to be on the go. I had to train myself, make myself to believe that I don't need to always be with someone to be happy. I don't need to break rules just to get my way. I don't need to lie about where I'm at when it's not necessary. As I sat in my room on a Friday evening, I remember thinking to myself, "How will you make it to the top? Because you have to make it by all means necessary." That line right there changed my life, changed how I thought. Right there at that very second, as I was thinking that thought, I knew that I was growing. Yes, it might have taken me a while, but I'm getting there, and turning back is not an option.

So I started writing goals on my mirror: reminding myself not to skip class, not to get sent out of class. Even when I thought about my grades, I just thought of one line that I made up, "A D is not acceptable, and Failing is not an option." They were just messages to keep me focused on what's important. So every morning, when I wake up, I see what I have to accomplish for the week. My mother gave me that idea, but when she first pitched it to me, I was still set in my rebel ways. My mother and father played a big part in my journey. Don't think I could have done it without either one of them. My mother showed me that life ain't always going be flowers and candy, showed me some true tough love. We got into a lot of arguments, fussing and fighting, but that made me grow, made me a stronger person. My father showed me that I don't always have to be on the go or be with friends to have a good time, and how I should focus myself more on school than gossip. The things they expressed to me put me in a bigger mind frame, made me wiser as a teen.

I think if they hadn't expressed to me how they felt and showed me some tough love, I wouldn't be as strong or wise as I am today.

In my future, I can see myself owning my own salon, checking up on it after I stay after school to help the kids on extra work or after I come from my private practice that I will be working at. Those are my visions, those are my goals.

As I sit here and write this paper, I look at what I was and what I am now. The girl I am today is much happier, knows where she's going, and knows some of the proper steps to get there. I now know that I will graduate on time and go to college to major in education and minor in journalism. I have the potential to own my own salon someday. I still continue to write my goals my mirror because like I stated before, I will make it to the top by all means necessary.

"As a young adult, I think about stuff like that and what to do better for my community and one day, how I can give back."

It's Not Impossible

Did you ever wonder how your life was going to be when you got older, like did you want to go to college in what you wanted to be when you got older or did you have things planned out? Well, I didn't, and now I'm a senior in high school. I attend Omaha South High School, and I don't know what I want to do when I graduate, but I have a clue. I want to go to college. Here a little something about me: I like to play sports such as basketball and football. I want to continue to play those in college and see how far they take me. When I was little, I used to play Pee Wee football for the Screaming Eagles. Playing basketball and football are my most favorite things to do. After college, I want to coach my own Pee Wee football team. I really don't know what I want to study in college, but Physical Education, Teaching and Coaching sound interesting.

Since I was little, my parents weren't really together. I was raised by my mother and family for a lot of my childhood. My mom had a hard time raising me without a father figure because she had my five sisters and four brothers to raise, too. Even though my mom had her hands tied, every day she made sure she cooked us a good meal, usually spaghetti and garlic. That's my favorite. Through my childhood, I also received lots of love from my grandpa, too. He supported me a lot at my football games when my mom had to work. When I looked up at the crowd at the games, my grandpa was easy to spot because of his cowboy hat. My relationship with my dad wasn't all that strong, but we did spend time bonding over the weekends playing video games, watching movies and we sometimes took fishing trips.

Later in life, I found me a girlfriend. She's amazing. Since I met her, things have been going good for me. We are usually always together. We spend lots of time outside of school hanging out, having fun or studying. When me and my girlfriend are not together, I'm usually with my best friend, Geo. We have some classes together, such as weight training and lunch. Outside of school, Geo and I do lots of stuff, like go to the movies together with our girlfriends. Recently, we just went to a haunted house called Scary Acres, but when we got there, Geo and the girls where scared. They transformed into some frightened kittens.

Where you come from in life can be important to you. That's where most of my hope comes from besides family. I grow up in a not-so-good neighborhood where you are most likely to not be successful in life. As a young adult, I think about stuff like that and what to do better for my community and one day, how I can give back.

Thoughts on Racism & Exclusion

"I began to see how the world really was and how if you don't know who you are, it can consume you and your life."

Too Little, Too Much

What's the first thing we see when we look at a person? Is it their face, body, or possibly their skin tone? Or do we see them as something much deeper than that, such as who they are and what experiences they have encountered? I mean, how many people do we know actually sit down to take the time out before they judge someone based on appearances? I do. I wonder about what each individual person's been through in order to make them who they are and to reach today. Once you know the truth about someone and the life they've lived, your thoughts seem shallow and judgmental right from the start ... Who knows what that person has been through? Or even who knows what you've been through and seen? All I know is what I've been through and experienced for my own pair of eyes.

Here I am today, my senior year in high school, really close to graduation and a start to a new life. It's time to start making wise decisions to base my life upon. Right now, you'd figure I'm just the everyday average American teen. Well, I am, but it wasn't always seen that way from past impressions and appearances, unwanted labels and stereotypes. Honestly, ever since I've been a child, I've hated stereotypes. They're just an easy way for people to categorize people they don't know or don't want to give time to know. But you can be so wrong about a person. For example, the really shy, quiet kid who stays to himself in your class may seem weird, but in reality and behind closed doors, something has happened to him to make him quiet and reserved. I guess what I'm trying to say is: how is it we judge people we haven't even given or want to give a chance to know?

Growing up as younger child, my memories weren't so vivid. All I can say is I do remember moving back and forth from home to home, school to school, and neighborhood to

229

neighborhood. The moment I started taking a grasp on my life, it seemed like things that were good would also change so suddenly. It was a little earlier than my preteen years when I began to see how the world really was and how if you don't know who you are, it can consume you and your life.

It was during those years I began to see how people can be mistreated for who they are and what they look like. See, I'm only half Mexican, and it was always brought to my attention one way or another how I didn't have enough in me, or how I didn't look like I was Mexican-American. Either way around it, I was. My father's a second generation Chicano, meaning he was born and raised in the United States. My father's mother was also born here, but my grandfather was born in Mexico. So that makes me third-generation Chicana, also born and raised here. It's outrageous how much we, as people, criticize whether we don't have enough Mexican, Caucasian, or African American in us. And the most shocking part of it all is it happens in every single race, not just one. If you're too light-skinned, you get teased, and if you're too dark, you also get teased. Is there ever a time when being ourselves is enough? I've sat and contemplated about a response and answer for that question. To be honest, as humans we cannot answer that. How I see it is: no one can define you but yourself.

I had to learn it the hard way, and it's even harder at a young age. It was around the fourth grade when I started to learn what racism was for myself, and not by being taught by the books in history class. It's amazing how, unknowingly, we can be under the mind control of racism. What's crazier is how it affects our youth, and they have no idea of what's going on in society today. As I think back, I'm pretty sure I was taught about Martin Luther King just a tiny bit after I started to understand the racism around me.

It was nothing new or uncommon for me to ever hear people state that I wasn't Mexican. You know, it actually happened a lot—perhaps every so often, to where I just got so tired of hearing it. I've heard it from just about every other person I know, including alleged friends and peers. I say "alleged" because I considered them a friend of mine, but how could they be a friend when all they seemed to ever do was bring up my race? I believe I was turned away and neglected by one side of my family because of my other nationality. In the past, it used to hurt and bother me because it was my family practically denying me. People get old, people grow up, and that's exactly what I did. I came to a realization and saw that I'm me. Either accept it or hate it. Either way, I have nothing to prove to anyone or need to change because I know who I am, what I stand for. It wouldn't be me losing out; it would be them losing a good thing.

As I think about it, the only person I've met who wasn't judgmental would be my grandmother. She's so genuine—like a pearl or diamond, I would say. Every time I see my grandma, she shows true affection, including her words and actions. She doesn't judge or criticize anyone. She takes them as they are and as they come, even if they mistreat her. That's why I love my grandma; she's like a saint to me, so precious and delicate. My grandpa and grandma have taken me places, gotten my family food, done special things for us without us asking. I feel as if my grandma puts my family's needs above her own sometimes. I once asked my mom how my grandma got to be so sweet because I know everyone has a story to how they became what they now are today. My mom's response was, "That's your grandma, and she's just always been that way!" I always get told I resemble my grandmother, and I don't mind how they say that; my grandma's a beautiful woman inside and out. I would like to get her open heart and free spirit as a person. It makes me feel so proud and blessed to hear I look like her, but I'm more proud to be her grandbaby and vice versa. I thank God for the grand-ma and grandpa He has given me; I couldn't ask for any better. I love my grandparents, and I know they love me, too. I wouldn't trade them for the world!

No one fully knows exactly what they are and where they originate from. There were so many explorers and invaders, too many to link back to a family tree. Even myself, I know I'm not only Mexican-American or Mexican and Caucasian, to show an example of how ignorant we can be even when it comes to knowing about ourselves. I recently discovered I have a tiny bit of Spanish history linked way back in my bloodline from genera-tions back. Somewhere in my genes, there's a relative who links far back to Spain. I'm unsure whether it is a man or woman, but all I do know they once existed. I wonder about the type of rac-ism they faced during their time, or even if they faced any? Was it similar to what we face today? I don't know if I'll ever know. It seems as if the history books skip over it. I don't know much about the person, but all I can say is I hope they were like my grandparents and had a warm heart. We all have stories like that. They may not be exactly similar, but we're all linked to some-thing, someone, and somewhere.

In the end, it shouldn't matter at all what race or national-ity we are, just what positive thing we may bring to the world and what difference we may make. It's wrong how people are so quick to judge or discriminate. Honestly, what is the importance? Does it make a person more special if they're more or less of a race? My thoughts on it are: no matter the race, we're all equal. We all have hopes and dreams. We all have backgrounds and family trees. My hopes are just that times continue to change for the best and not for the worst. We've come a long way and too far from the Dr. King movement to stop now and lose everything he and the men and women before us had worked for. So, all I ask is for people not to be so quick to judge and be critical. To the ones facing what many of us have once faced and still face today, only you and God know what you've been through. Therefore, only God can pass judgment upon us. Just remember: you don't need to prove yourself to anyone; just be you and no one else.

*"We came here
for a dream.
I wish this dream
could be available
to everyone."*

Hope and Opportunities Should Be For Everyone

One of the thousands of reasons I came here was because I was tired of seeing my Mom crying while my brother and I were out of food and clothing. She was a very sick woman, hurt, and I just was a young girl of seventeen years who had no control of her own life, so I decided to change my situation and also show that love is not just a word—you need demonstrate it to people who you love.

When I crossed the border, it wasn't easy because we were six women and seventeen men. I was the youngest and I was afraid because I didn't know what would happen to me. I remember very well those days, often wishing I could forget. But ultimately I have to remind myself why I'm here and for whom.

That day was September 16 of 2008, and we were ready to begin our journey to the north. Before we left, we prayed to *La Virgen* of Guadalupe to guide us in our travels to cross the border. When we reached the Sinaloa/Arizona border, an immense wall of nine feet or more was blocking our hopes and dreams. The fear of breaking my leg or even dying crossed my mind.

The difficulty of our task was that twenty-three of us needed to climb in ten minutes without leaving footprints in the earth because the American police could discover us, but thanks to God, everyone made it across and we started our trip walking, guided by *La Virgen*.

Many thoughts cross my mind during our walk. I thought about the family, pets, and friends that I left behind without saying goodbye. I didn't know if I would to see them again.

By nightfall all was well, but I never thought it could be so cold; I just had on jeans and a shirt with long sleeves. At dusk, it began to rain and we had nowhere to go, so we stayed in the bushes. The coyote said we could not continue, but we did not want to stop. It would only get colder as the night went on. What we didn't know was the coyote was already lost.

Everyone was asleep by 11 p.m. I swear the cold was like a thousand knives cutting my skin. It was the worst night of my life. My clothes and hair were wet by the rain. I never thought I would want to cry so much and not be able to do it because my tears would freeze just as my hair did. At that moment I missed the warm arms of my Mommy when she hugged me when I was sick or sad. I regretted leaving the people who I love most in this world, but it was necessary for my success and survival. When I was under the bushes, I just thought, "I have to survive." When you are a single woman, you need to prepare your mind. I hugged myself and the other women to keep the little heat that we could. That night was the coldest, longest and saddest of all my life.

When we started out again at 5 a.m., I prayed to God to give us strength to go on for however long. We were six women with seventeen good men. They never tried to do anything dangerous.

The next day was very different. We went from being so cold to feeling like we were dying of heat and dehydration. With no water available, many of the men took of their sweaty shirts and wrung them out to drink. We found a dirty pond, and we took some of that water to try to clean ourselves and to drink. We thanked God because we just wanted to drink anything that we could get. We also were angry because the coyote was saying we would arrive soon and that we would have to face walking for two days without changes.

At 2 p.m., the coyote left us under some trees and said he would return with water. But five hours passed, and we were scared because we thought we had been abandoned in the desert. Thankfully, he returned to tell us that the truck was ready, and we were all so happy. After another hour the truck arrived, and we ran toward it. I was squashed behind the driver's seat underneath two women. I was crying in pain, and I couldn't imagine how the seventeen men in the back were feeling.

Pain, loss, struggle, despair and courage are feelings that I share with my boyfriend's cousin, who came to Omaha to find a life that was not only better but also safer. It was when she got to Mexico from Honduras that her difficulties started. The train she was riding was stopped by Mexican troops. Everyone escaped and started running. She ran for ten minutes and found herself lost. She went up to a house she thought had immigrants, but that was the worst mistake she could make. In those moments when you try to seek help, you're not thinking about possible danger. The man told her that she could come in and relax since she was frantic. She thought he was a good person since he let her eat and bathe.

Once she was relaxed, the night arrived, and he would not let her use the phone. That's when she saw seven men and six women coming up to the house. She became scared of the goon, and he said she had better not ask anything if she wanted to stay alive. She begged to be let go, but he would not allow her to leave. The men who arrived were evil and disgusting. She was raped, beaten, and drugged for a week. Then the old bastard opened the door to let her go, and she ran as if she were breathing for the first time. She still had strength and hope and did not give up; those men had not taken everything from her. She found a work in Chetumal, Quintanaroo, and when she earned enough money after a month, she communicated with her family who put her in contact with the coyote.

She arrived safely in Omaha and was reunited with her family. Her family had to sacrifice everything they had in Honduras. They sold all their valuable belongings, including their home and animals, to raise the money to come to the U.S. Crossing the border from Honduras cost about $7,000, but it was worth it to her family to have a better, safer life.

We came here for a dream. I wish this dream could be available to everyone. Sometimes I don't understand the minds of many Americans or even Mexican Americans who are racist. I find myself asking, why they do want to send me back? What did I do to them? I just came to go to school, I do my volunteer work, and my family donates when we can. And they still hate me because I'm Mexican.

Sometimes I wish to die because I don't want to see how the world is destroyed gradually by selfishness and envy. People focus on being beautiful and rich, but the most beautiful are those who are good in the heart and mind.

I tell my stories to others because I have suffered and cried. I will do everything to change people's minds who are different and not selfish. My wishes and my hopes are not only mine, but also those of Latino students around me. We want to overcome, but we cannot do it alone. We need you Americans as support. I am not an expert in the English language, but I have opportunities to work and feel safe here, and I'm grateful for that and for the support of the Susan Buffet Scholarship and the other public scholarships and people who help us.

Because of my experiences, I'm a person who does take risks. I know that if I do not risk difficult things, I will never know if they could have benefitted me. No matter what happens, I'll know that at least I tried. The winner knows that victory depends on herself while the loser believes in bad luck, and I'm not a loser. I know that life is love, and I live because I have a purpose—to fight for the right of any Latino person who lives in the U.S. to get the same opportunities as anyone who wants to overcome in this country.

Let me tell you what is really important: God gives us a certain amount of money to live, but the rest of the money that's leftover is just to show off. If I get a lot of money, I will buy my family a house and make sure they never have to worry about paying bills. And then I will still work helping others, because then I will have purpose, even if I don't have to work. It is important to help others because I think God tells us to love not just those who love you, but also those who don't. In Spanish it's *cadena*—a chain. When you do good for someone, they can go on to do good for others. We don't need to wait to receive something in return from the people we help.

Who said that everything in life is easy?

"Just because something is difficult doesn't mean I shouldn't try — it means I will just have to try harder."

Becoming the Hope for Others

In Fremont, Nebraska, the immigrant people can't rent houses or apartments because they don't have social security numbers. If this law passes to Omaha, Nebraska, it will affect my uncle, because he doesn't have documents. He is an important person who loves his daughter. She is a ten-year-old girl who he wants to see but can't. This endangers his human rights because he's not being treated as an equal human being. And this would affect my family if this law passes to Omaha by affecting our relationship with him. Already, when we go to Mexico, he feels upset because he can't go, and it makes me upset, too. Another way this would affect our family is if he gets caught. We can get into trouble or have problems, too.

The businesses are also affected by anti-immigrations laws. They lose money because they can't rent to immigrants, and companies are losing workers. There are people willing to work, but they can't because they lack the correct documentation.

My uncle has been working for seven years, and he is an important person in our lives. He sends money to Mexico because he just wants a better life for his daughter, so she can have a better life than he had. I want to make a difference for these immigrants. I believe that the people responsible for this do have hearts; however, I think they should set aside their preconceived ideas and listen with their hearts to how these people feel—like how my family and I feel about this law. This law is unfair for everyone who is an immigrant, as well as for legal people.

If I were someone important who could contribute a voice to this debate, I would help all people no matter what. I would fight to help them. Just because we have brown skin (or another color) doesn't mean that we are criminals. Just because we are Latinos or Hispanics doesn't mean we're trying to break the law.

My heart has been broken into pieces since this law passed in Fremont, Nebraska. Some people will think that I'm being insincere, but they don't see the tragedies that I see happening because of this law: families torn apart, good people suffering, and so on.

Last time I talked with my mom, she told me that if this law passes to Omaha, Nebraska, that we can't do anything about it right now, but we shouldn't stop fighting. She means everything to me. She is so special, and she helps me see what's right and wrong. She is my life, and I don't know what's going to happen if I lose her someday. I told her that when I grow up, I want to be an immigration lawyer and help people in need—people in the same situations as my uncle and me.

When I graduate from law school, I will have more education and more power to be heard so that I can help immigrant people and could protect them. I will help them to get documents and fight for their rights to be treated as equal human beings. Graduating from the university will be special to me and for my family, too. I will be a professional helping the immigrant people, and my mom will be so proud of me because I will be the first to go to the university and have a professional job. Graduating from university will be a dream come true, but changing people's minds is going to be difficult. However, just because something is difficult doesn't mean I shouldn't try—it means I will just have to try harder.

*"Just think about it;
it's stupid that we're
judging people more
by their color than
by their character."*

The Dream

My hope for the future is that one day, we won't have racism in this great big world. It's unbelievable how this goes on in my everyday life. There are many things that happen to me, and I just want to get to express my feelings!!

May 10, 2010: It's the high school boy's state soccer final. It's amazing how the boys from Omaha South are here. But there's one thing standing in the way of their very first state championship, and that's the Lincoln East boys—the undefeated dream team. But South had one thing that they didn't, and that was their amazing community behind them through thick and thin. Let's go, boys! The whistle blows and the game starts.

There are over seven thousand people in the stands and people waiting outside to get in. We blew the old record for attendance for a high school sport or anything in Omaha. The game started. Twenty minutes in, a threw ball from my boy Guero to Alex. We scored. Then, East scores right after. It's 1-1, and the first half is over. The second half starts. East scores, so they're up with 2 minutes left and bam! My boy Agustin rips a shot. Upper 90. Yeah, buddy! The final whistle blows, and the game is tied 2-2. Overtime, baby! Oh, *bleep*! East scores in the first five minutes. South's hopes drop. The final whistle blows. The boys drop to their knees with tears falling from their faces. That's when you see the East fans rush the field, and what looks like green confetti gets thrown up into the dark, black sky. As I see the cards drop, I walk over, pick one of them up and realize it isn't confetti. They're "green" cards—a racist joke saying, "Go back to Mexico; you're never going to be better than us." It gets to us, but we hold our heads high and walk off the field with our prides hurt.

The next day at school, it was crazy how much support

we got from our classmates and teachers. There were so many reporters that came to the school wanting to interview us and see how we felt. Only a couple of us got to speak, but I think those who did really represented the rest of us really well. The captain of the team really explained how we felt and how this wasn't the first time this has happened; it's in our everyday life, too. We were hurt, but we've learned how to forgive and forget. That's just how we were raised. It was crazy, like we were even on Telemundo—an international Spanish news channel—so the whole world knew about what happened in Omaha, Nebraska, on May 10, 2010.

That's why I'm writing about this—to get the word out. It's crazy how we're in 2010, and there's still stuff like this going on. It makes me sad and ashamed. It's kind of hard to keep my head up when every time I try to do something good, someone has to pull the racist card. It's like the day at the mall when I realized that the security guard was following me and my friends. It makes me mad and kind of sad. It's like, "*Come on*. Do you really have to follow me because I'm colored? Why aren't you following the white group? It's cause you group all of us together, and just cause I'm Mexican, you must follow me? Ha ha. It's funny to me now because I'm so used to it. You're just wasting your time because I'm buying all of my stuff." Sometimes I just want to turn around and be like, "Can I help you with something? Can I ask why you're following me?"

It's crazy how people fought for their freedom back in the day and for us to still be pulling this racist card the way we do. We should be ashamed. Just think about it; it's stupid that we're judging people more by their color than their character. Just give me a chance before you judge me, and then and only then you can say the truth about how you feel. But I know if I had the chance to prove to you that I'm not what you think I am and I *still* can't change your mind, oh well. It might affect me, but at the end of the day, I know that only God can judge me.

It's weird how some people pull the racist card because when you're little, you really don't care, and you are friends with everyone. The little kids that I train to play the great game of soccer remind me of those days. We all can learn from them. They're all different colors, but that doesn't matter to them. They're best of friends on the field and even off the field. They see each other as they really are, not the color of their skin. I wish that one day while I'm still alive that there won't be any more racism in this great big world. I'm giving back because soccer always gave to me, and I hope that soccer can give back to these little ones. Well, my dad got me into soccer, and it's crazy how he was only one month away from playing pro ball, but his mom got sick. He always told me that it just wasn't meant to be. He loved soccer, and he made me love it, too. He told me that this is my ticket to get out of Omaha and onto better things. He said, "Soccer is always gonna be there for you," and it always has. I can get my mind off of anything if I just touch a ball; soccer is such a great sport. Hopefully, soccer will get me somewhere. My dad took care of me, and pretty soon, it's going to be my turn to take care of him. When these little kids are playing and I see their smiles, it makes me forget about all the racist stuff going on in this world. It makes me want to tell everyone, "Why can't we be like them and forget what color we are and see people for their personality?" I hope that contributing to these little kids helps everyone to eventually come around. I see myself in the future getting a job that focuses on soccer or that makes me work with many people, and I hope by me doing something, it can change the minds of millions.

We've come far, but we still have a lot left to go. Twenty years ago, my parents moved here, and there were only a couple

Mexicans that lived here. My dad had to learn English real quick to get a job. Little by little, more and more colored people moved here to Omaha. Now I'm 17, and there's a bunch of colored people here, and racism is still there but slowly going away. We've worked hard to get here, and slowly it's paying off. It feels good that this little problem is going away. Hopefully, before I die, it will have gone away.

Once again, my hope for the future is that there won't be any racism in this great big world!! Just get to know me. Give me one chance before you judge me. Have one conversation with me before you decide to say something about me or even judge me, and just maybe by you talking with me, *just maybe* I can change your mind about me. I'm not just talking about Mexicans but everyone. We should just give them a chance. We once were all immigrants to this great country. Not only you, but all of us who call home the United States of America!!

"People can teach, upset, love, damage, and serenade each other. These things make life real."

Hope, People, Bananas, Life

Hope. One syllable. Just another four-letter word. What could that offer? To me, it offers quite a bit to be skeptical of. Then, when I think about what makes love, faith, and understanding possible, I can't help but think that hope is that very thing.

And without people, there'd be nothing to hope in, nothing to hope for. Humans are made to interact. And from every moment that fizzes out, explodes, or lets off a blinding toxic gas that lingers, comes a moment that sparkles, that heals, that brings together two incomplete substances to make something wonderful. I live for those interactions. My hope is in people.

Hope is something different to every person, and there are millions of answers to the question: What does hope do for you? Hope has a list of benefits as long as the number of people planning to live to see tomorrow. Hope is comfort. Hope is something to hold onto, but only metaphorically. Hope can only keep a person going; what they do decides where they're heading. For some, hope is a lifeline. People are hoping their families aren't destroyed, that they will live to see tomorrow, and that they will have a chance to better the lives of those around them. For others, hope is a luxury. People are hoping to get home in time for the latest hit series and hoping to, someday soon, get paid the big bucks.

I would say that "hope," as a word, is whimsical. It seems to fit into stories better than it fits into life. People usually hope for fairy tale endings, while life brings off-white horses carrying scrawny princes. Hopes are for smiles and springtime. In reality though, half the smiles hide pain and springtime brings a lot of rain. People hope to be happy, but when's the last time that emotions could neatly fold into *that* five-letter drawer? Life is heavy, and life takes strength. And "hope" can appear light and impractical.

As only a word, hope doesn't impress me much at all. It doesn't move me or seem to hold any power. Sometimes people offer me hope, suggest that I get some hope—for the future, for peace, for good weather—and I politely decline. Motivation, rapture, longing, passion and wholeheartedness are ideas that tug at my heart and sway my feelings and invigorate my actions. I really try not to hope in the future because the behavior I've seen stemming from that is over-ambitious, over-zealous and over-expectant. How many opportunities are left unconsidered when one single-mindedly pursues a solitary prospect? How many people, places, and experiences are passed by now for something that might appear later? It wouldn't make sense to look at all the bananas on a grocery store shelf, never taking any home because there might be better looking bananas tomorrow. What if an anti-banana extremist group blew up all the banana delivery trucks in your area, or in the world? You may never have another chance to start a morning off right with that sweet yellow fruit, conveniently packaged in its own happy, yellow peel. Now, it may seem like I'm comparing apples and oranges, but the way I see it, while the future may be full of possibilities, the present is full of opportunities.

As for hoping in the past, it's like betting on a game that was already played. This makes me think of Sandy Lyle, played by Philip Seymour Hoffman in *Along Came Polly*. This guy played bagpipes in a movie as a kid and every once in a while, someone would recognize him. Sandy would ask if they'd like an autograph and they'd decline, but as a middle-aged man, he's still a star in his own mind. I don't want my life to be like that, based on what already happened. What I did is never going to matter again as much as it did while I was experiencing it. My past may shape who I am, but what I do now is what defines me. And with people, every moment counts, but only while it's happening. You may know someone's yesterday, but all you've got there is history. I want to hope in the instant I'm living in and cherish the people I'm living with.

So, even though humans keep hurting and the chance of getting struck by lightning is higher than the chances of winning the lottery, I have decided that what life has to offer every moment of every day is worth being here for. I think of Matthew 6:34: "Therefore do not worry about tomorrow, for tomorrow will worry about itself. Each day has enough trouble of its own." And actually, I think, "trouble" could be swapped for a term to suit any circumstance, e.g. "fun", "confusion", "jokes", "cake", etc. And I am satisfied to share whatever a day dishes out with those around me, especially if it's cake.

Speaking of cake, I love people. Speaking of people, I love what's human, and I hope in what's real. There's a lot of stuff out there telling people what's generally right and acceptably true. Parents, religion, media, friends, and society in general all give us rules. I hope in the parts of people that want to find out what life is about for them and what works for their own relationships. I hope in the parts of people that look for more and do things because they love life and they love others. I will always have hope that every single person is worth living for and hoping in. Every person has a story worth hearing and every person is more than a lifetime can discover.

I've hoped in so many things that are beyond my control. I've hoped in the past to make sense and the future to be clear. I've hoped in the concept of family to be strong enough to hold mine together. I've hoped for my heart to be able to break for others without spilling me all over. I've hoped for a god to have a plan and for blueprints in the sky. I've hoped in knowing more

and forgetting more and forgiving more and being more careful.
I've hoped in people to show me the impossible and I've wished
myself to do what I couldn't. I've hoped that I wouldn't be let
down and I never wanted to disappointment anyone.
Many people have been subjected to my mixed-up hopes. When
someone I'd hoped in failed, I'd add a mark to the tally of reasons it was an impossibility that I would ever succeed in anything. Whenever I would take up a pencil and paper, I couldn't
help but to try and work out what this life, and all I had learned
to hope for, added up to. And what all of it was worth always
emerged as a negative number.

Well, that's how those explosions of toxic gas can feel, right?
I felt like hope was sort of passive aggressive. Anyway, I suppose
if other hopes hadn't failed me, I might not have found myself
where I am today. I may not have found my hope in people.

One day, I hurt somebody. Well, that part wasn't new, but
this person was hurt by my hurt. Through all the walls I built
and the mask I thought was pretty deceptive, but someone saw
me. She cried all the tears I had held in and gave words to the
things I didn't know how to say yet.

At the time, I felt terrible and I felt helpless. She couldn't
stop crying, and I couldn't break the habit of holding back my
tears. She wanted to say the perfect words, and I could have told
her anything except what I was feeling. Her heart was in front
of me, breaking for me. And what hurts the most is that she
couldn't see that my heart mirrored hers.

And the hope that she had in love and in people and in God,
and the hope she had in me came rushing in. She gave me so
much more than she thought I took. I was torn open and the
warped expectations, inevitable regret, and unrelenting melan-
choly that I had mistaken for life were rapidly deflating. And it
took me a while to realize it, but that's when hope's role in my

life redefined itself.

As an excuse, the past has expired, and I certainly can't blame what's still to come for what hasn't yet been done. Each moment holds only what is happening, and all I have is the wonderful freedom of living here and now. I don't need to be anything in particular, and what the future may hold, it can keep. People can save people. People can teach, upset, love, damage, and serenade each other. These things make life real. People make hope real.

So, what are my hopes and plans? I hope to live every second that I'm alive, and I plan to plan on people being silly, unreasonable, strong, vulnerable, beautiful, inconsistent and persistent. I expect truth to come in contradictions. And I hope to never lose hope. I imagine that I will have doubts, fears, and tribulations. But as long as I have people, I will hope.

Fun Things They Love

"While I talk about hope
for myself, it's not
the same for the people
I've seen who have
lost their hope.
Maybe they didn't
lose it, but
they buried it."

Slipping Through the Cracks of Hope

Music is my life's playlist. Music is my life and my air, because every song connects to who I am as a person. And that's hope, which means don't ever forget who you really are and what makes you, you. Mexico is home for me. Maybe I wasn't born there, but Mexico reminds me that my life could be very different if my family had not decided to immigrate to the States. But going "home" means that I could stand in the doorway of my grandmother's house and smell the raw earth, reminding me of Adam and Eve, how they were created and the hopes that God had for them and for the human race. It reminds me of the hopes my parents had for me. In the courtyard of my *abuelita's casa*, on wash days, we would hang the clothes on lines and let the bright, strong sun dry them, as Americans would say, 'the old fashioned way.' The air was so sweet, and it smelled of fresh clothes that your mom has just taken out, but cleaner somehow. And they had such a clean smell that I could only try to describe, for they were mostly my *abuelita's* clothes, which had a smell like rich peppermint, the raw earth, and medicinal sweets—the smell of a hard life. I still dream of that smell and of those memories, and I wake up crying because it reminds me of the hard life that my grandmother led and that she never wanted her children or grandchildren to ever lead. Through my *abuelita*, through the hope that she carried for everyone in her family, my hope stems from her. She's played a huge role in my life, even to now, and I don't think that I will ever be able to find words to explain how much I credit the memory of my *abuelita* for the person I am now. My hope that life wasn't as hard as it seemed, which is why the playlist for this part of my life would have to include *Shadow Of The Day* by Linkin Park.

Still Around by 3Oh!3 is the next song of my life. Like all good things that eventually come to an end, once my family immigrated here three or so years before I was born, they, just like every single immigrant before them, realized how cold and harsh the reality of it really was. My parent's expectations to come here were to give us children the world. America filled them, along with all immigrants, with an illusion that people are nice, you will get a job right away, and that you will earn lots of money quickly.

It was a false sense of hope. And maybe that's why, when my brother got sick (and even before that), they put all their dreams and hopes into me. My father had always wanted to be a doctor, dreamed of it even. But because of family issues and him having to step up and be the man of the household, his dreams went unrealized. Maybe that's why my parents have wanted me to become the picture-perfect daughter who lived out their dreams. I'm sad for my parents because while I would love to have become their image of this girl they expected me to be, I can only say that I have turned out to be the person who I'm meant to be, instead of some cardboard copy clone that I see so many others being. I understand that they accept me for who I have become, I just think that they have not accepted many of the choices I have made within my life. Maybe they had all these expectations that society said I could grow up and become, but I won't make their dreams become all truth. I'll still be their daughter, and I think that's the only thing they want for me.

My parents have taught me to fight for what I believe in and be the person I *want* to become. But isn't that true for all parents? Parents expect a lot, yet when their child grows up and becomes someone quite different, they are disappointed yet happy at the very least because their child has chosen to live the way that best suits them. This is something that I've realized, and it's something that's true to me. Even still, all the sacrifices that have been made for me are enough to always remind me that one day, I will go back to Mexico and remember that it all started somewhere. *I* started somewhere.

R.I.P. by 3Oh!3 is a song that explains why I want to get out of this town so bad. I may never forget where I came from, but I still want to live my life the way I want to live it. Whenever in my life that I can, I want to travel to Japan. I want to live there because I have always felt as though I was born into the wrong culture. The Mexican heritage isn't quite the culture for me. It suits someone other than me. I don't fit the mold that comes with being of this heritage, though I got the fate that was dealt to me, and I'm okay with it either way. I've learned to accept that, for whatever reason, I was born into a specific culture, though that doesn't mean I can't adopt another culture or adapt myself into that culture. I always wonder if there's a word for that, and I think the word would have to be trans-culture. I want to go to South Korea and Japan and *really* find myself, really know if what I've always thought about these two cultures is a somewhat correct assumption. The music and the food and the clothes and the culture are all things that I truly love and sort of understand, including the language now that I'm more or less learning it. I've always said that things like music and culture are universal, but they are only universal if and only if people find out about them. Maybe I don't belong in the culture, but it's a culture that I want to adapt myself into. I want to be accepted—something I know that may never happen—but it's what I want. I'm prepared to be disappointed if it ends differently. Sorta like that book *Eat, Pray, Love*, just without the praying. It's a silly comparison, but it fits who I feel I am anyway. I know the cultures are different, incredibly different, but it's a culture that I can understand. It's one that I know the best. I don't have to act like something I'm not just to be accepted; silly how that worked out. Maybe I have no true culture, but I have a sense of who I am, at least.

Remember Me by Birthday Massacre and *Automatic* by Tokio Hotel are the songs I have to feel are for some of the people I see who lose have their hope. Because while I talk about hope for *myself*, it's not the same thing for the people I've seen who have lost their hope. Maybe they didn't lose it, but they buried it. To me, that would be like someone telling me that they had to take music away from my life. I would feel dead, not real, not of this world. To me, losing hope would be like not being the real me. Maybe it's something like how I believe that I'm going to get out of this town one day. It's like so many women of my culture that I've seen who just look out their windows, and, as stated by Esperanza from *The House On Mango Street*: "… the others who lay their necks on the threshold waiting for the ball and chain." I'm afraid of becoming that way. I think about it and wonder, *When will that happen to me? When will I finally realize that there is no place for me and grow up, move somewhere close to my family, and learn how to bury my hope?* The truth is, I don't think that will ever happen, yet I am so afraid of becoming exactly what society expects of me. Isn't it ironic that when someone doesn't want to become something, they end up becoming exactly what they most dreaded? I want to know that even if I do ever get married and when I become a mother, I can support myself and my children. And yet, sometimes thinking about the future makes me worry about all the "what ifs." Which is why, on days when I think about those "what ifs" I can be mean. I'm not nice to anyone at all, because I only want to think and not have anyone disturb my thoughts. I know it's wrong, I'm not going to try and justify my actions with some pathetic excuse of how I don't know it's wrong. It's just that I can't seem to make myself quit. I want so much to escape the mold that has been thrown into my face almost from the beginning and become someone that I know won't fit the mold that I should fit. Maybe that's why, to this day, I still can't seem to have many friends of my own race, simply because I don't feel like we have anything at all in common. I don't want to get stuck in a land that kills your dreams and tells you, *It's time to grow up. Put away the dreams and lets hope that maybe your children can live them.*

Sunset Glow by the Korean pop band Big Bang is a song that may not have anything do with my hope, but it still lifts me up. It's one of those songs that just lifts you up the minute it starts playing. While finding myself and getting unstuck are my hopes, maybe none of that matters. Maybe none of this matters. Maybe, in the end, all I can ever hope for is to be the best I can ever be. I remember a memory from my 8th grade Art class. It was just one of those regular days where we did something basic, really not so very artsy to me. But I remember looking up at the wall and noticing for the first time a poster that must have been there the entire year. The poster had only a simple quote against a black background, and it said, "Life is like a music sheet. From the minute you are born, to the minute you die, you start to compose the way YOU want to compose and the way YOU want to play it…And at the end of your life…you have to be happy with the way you left your painting and finally sign your name at the bottom to prove to yourself that you were once here." I have no idea, why, now, some four years later, that quote has still stuck with me, but it reminds me of this other quote that I read somewhere else:

What happens if your choice is misguided?
You must try to correct it.
But what if it's too late? What if you can't?
Then you must find a way to live with it.

Isn't that what we all strive to do everyday? Not just me,

but the person down the street. Or the person who walks down the hall with no real friends, or the one with no friends at all. We have to live with the choices we've made, and sometimes it's easier said than done. But little by little, we learn to accept such things and move on with life. That's not to say that I think we have to resign ourselves to our fates, but only that while Fate or God or whoever you want to believe in can control your destiny, you have a say in it, too. I know that I do have a say in how my life—my *music sheets*—ends out as. I think, that all I want, all I truly, truly want is to die with my hope still alive. I don't care if I'm a bucket of ashes inside of some urn somewhere. I just want to leave this world knowing that someone is carrying on my hope for me. Because all my life, I've felt as though I wasn't born the right way, but I've always had hope that maybe, just maybe, there are people out there who think the same way and who can live out my hope for me. Because all I can ever hope to be is myself. There's no right way of living, so shouldn't I live my life the way I think I should, even if they way I live is entirely taboo and not what people expect? I find surprising people entertaining anyway, and I've always felt that I should leave this world with a bam!

So, you know what book makes me cry? *The Diary of Anne Frank*, because of that huge sense of hope that reaches even me. Because now ... we're at the end. And the perfect songs to end this are *Airplanes* by B.O.B. featuring Hayley Williams and Eminem and *Always* by Big Bang. The first is understandable, and the second would have to be because I just love that song. Some of you must have cried buckets reading this little essay of some unimportant girl or you just skimmed it wanting to get to the better stories. At least, I got my voice out there. Hope is my life though, and it's something that has such a strong impact. I'm not trying to make you cry. I'm not trying to make you mad. I'm simply trying to get my viewpoint of the world around me across to someone else, maybe someone in another country, maybe someone of a different religion or a different culture! I want my voice to be heard loud and clear, because so many people who I have seen will never get the same chance. If I can get my voice heard, maybe someone, somewhere will realize that it's *okay*. It's okay what you're feeling and what you're thinking because, guess what?! I'm in the same boat with you! But you won't know that. What if you see me walking down the hall and you don't even know that you just read my story? Would you notice me? Maybe your thoughts would be centered around the fact that I didn't look like the ideal type, but you wouldn't know that. Would you stop me on the street? Let's say, just for pure laughs, that you're some superstar or even just a regular person walking down the street who probably never even heard my story (Or maybe you have. Who knows, really?). Would you stop me if you knew? Would you look at me and wonder what were my dreams, my hopes, my passions, and defeats? Would you stop me if I seemed like a caring person? Would you even care? Would you react any differently if you suddenly realized what it is that I think about? Would you?

"Just because I'd rather wear a sneaker than a heel or jeans before a skirt doesn't make me a tomboy at all."

A Day in the Life of a Pair of Jordans

On October 26, 2013, I will buy my 100th pair of Air Jordans.

That will show a sign of my independence, personality, and hard work. I love shoes and will do whatever it takes to get them. When I wear my Jordans, I feel like Superwoman. I'm the main attraction; I'm invincible. I can count on myself to get what I want and need and to do what I need to do.

In the summer of 2009, I went to Champs and bought my first pair. They were high top Retro 1's with laser/teal blue polka dots and black suede with white stitching. The Nike swoosh on them was what convinced me to purchase those shoes. I worked really hard, and for all that labor, I got to buy the shoes I really wanted. My motivation to work so hard is for the things I want. I was proud of myself. I continued this attitude as I pushed myself to work harder for what I wanted. I absolutely love being independent. It makes me feel good to know that I can get something on my own, and I'll be able to say it, too.

Shoes are really cool to me. I love them, especially Jordans. A guy named London Trotter really influenced me to start purchasing Jordans. He has so many and taught me a lot about them and the importance of shoes. It's because of him that I know all the numbers of the Retros that have come out and been released in local stores. It's crazy because I never was very interested in buying sneakers at all. I thank him for introducing me to Jordans. I actually liked them and will keep buying them in the future. These shoes are very spectacular to me; I adore them.

A unique shoe to me has to be colorful, yet plain, dull, yet sharp. There are so many different kinds of shoes that come in different shapes and sizes. It's quite amazing to me because even though Michael Jordan has retired, in every game he played, he wore a pair of Jordans. Why not do the best and be seen in the best? Every game. He is so cool to me. His wife divorced him and took half his money, and he is still rich. That didn't slow him down a bit. He kept on going. He reminds me of myself so much, being able to snap back from something tragic so soon is major and a blessing. He is strong and didn't cry over spilled milk. He cleaned it up and kept pushing. When I lost my job, I didn't give up; I kept going as well. I also was in a group home, just like Michael Jordan, and look at us now. I don't see how he did it, just carrying on after being heartbroken the way he was. I don't think I could handle that or take it the way Jordan did. I'm going to be just like him. I'll come from nothing and make something out of myself. I think I'll be famous and rich just like him. I know that to become rich one day, I will need to work hard and finish my school. Education is a *must*. The more education you have, the more money you make. Also, the more bragging rights you have.

Shoes are more than just shoes to me. I clean them, pamper them, and take very good care of them, as if they were a vehicle or maybe even a human being. Taking care of your personal items is very good. Every time I take off a pair of my shoes, I clean them thoroughly. I do that so that when I wear them the next time, they look as good as new. I organize them in alphabetical order so I know where to look for them, and it also helps me figure out what I'll wear the following day. I love being neat. I feel as if whatever you own, you must take excellent care of it no matter what. I wouldn't have it any other way. My feet have grown quite a bit, so shoe size for me is a bit different. However, the prices are the same. That's the best part about it. The smaller your feet are, the less expensive your shoes will be. I love it!!

My shoes mean a lot to me. A boy I know named Juan tried trying on my shoes, and I told him, "Do it, and it'll be World

War 3." That's how serious I was about my sneakers. Asking me to wear my shoes is like asking my to borrow my undergarments; it's not just going to happen. No way. I look up to Mr. Jordan because he has conquered a whole lot. He has worked very hard to get where he is. I want to be just like him when I grow up. Mr. Jordan makes lots and lots of money for his products—not only shoes but clothing as well. I think to myself, "Wow, he really is the best."

To me it is clear that I have a shopping problem. I remember I used to spend my whole check on only Jordans. It appeared to be a problem. I looked at it as treating myself for how hard I had to work. I sometimes wonder how much money Michael Jordan makes from people buying his products. Mr. Jordan raised his prices, and the people still are buying these shoes. It's unbelievable to me. I think to myself, "What a smart guy." I wish I could do that.

I'm often mistaken for tomboy because of my fetish for sneakers. I feel as if there's nothing wrong with the way I dress. I love it. Just because I'd rather wear a sneaker than a heel or jeans before a skirt doesn't make me a tomboy at all. I'm perfectly fine. The way a person wears their shoes can reveal a lot about them, as far as their personality, tidiness, if they are plain or colorful, or if they're boring or fun. To me, if a person always dresses with dark colors or lots of tattoos, you can about guess what they're going through.

When I buy my 100th pair of shoes, that is going to be so amazing to me. I will have to have a celebration. Celebrations can be great. I love them because they are so colorful and joyful. They make me feel alive and outgoing. Everything and everyone is happy and full of laughter. My shoes tell a lot about me. I am a changed young lady, and I'm very happy with myself and those around me. I sort of express myself through my shoes and the majority of the time, I wear my mood. I am totally different from the girl I used to be. I am phenomenal and very bright. I love myself. I wouldn't have it any other way. I'm thankful. And that's what a celebration is all about to me—love, joy, happiness, loving yourself first and being grateful for what you have achieved.

Afterword
The Teacher's Perspective

by Ferial Pearson
English Teacher, Omaha South High Magnet School

When I first became a teacher, I had no idea how much I would be getting out of my vocation. I thought that I would be the one to impart knowledge and experiences from my students and that I would enrich their lives somehow, but it turns out that the opposite happens every single day. I have learned that teenagers have a lot to say, a lot to teach me and the rest of the world, and a lot of experiences from which we all can learn.

Two years ago, I had a group of students in my sophomore English class who didn't particularly care about reading and writing, and some voiced extreme displeasure at the thought of poetry. Some of the boys pouted and said poetry was for girls. Others wondered what on earth they would get out of reading poetry, much less writing it. I wondered how to get them interested and decided to try bringing in some of their own experiences and language in the classroom. I found Hip Hop poetry and the Spoken Word. I found bilingual poetry, and poetry by adolescents. We read it, listened to it, and watched it being performed by nationally known slam poets.

The result was exciting; students performing in slam poetry jams at the beginning of every class period, there was discussion of poetic terminology, tons of revision, and, last but not least, seventeen students published in a local literary journal called *Fine Lines* which was just what they needed. For some of them, it turned their lives around and kept them in school. They took writing more seriously knowing that there could be a real audience and some kept on writing and being published even

271

after they were done with my class. They received fan mail from people who had read their poetry. One student, who had been ready to drop out of school at that time, has been published four times and has even gone on to start a poetry group at the local Boys and Girls Club where he teaches younger children how to write their own poetry. These students are now seniors, and you have just read their essays.

The greatest moments in my career as an educator come when students take what they have learned from the classroom and use it in their own lives. I teach from the perspective of social justice. Everything that happens in my classroom is under an umbrella; to facilitate freedom, empowerment, hope, and change in my students' lives and in their communities. Writing plays a huge part in this for many reasons. They use their journals as confidantes and places to work out their problems, but they also use their writing to inform, entertain, educate, change, and most importantly, hope.

When I met Alli Lopez and heard about the Omaha Young Writers Project during the summer of 2010, I knew that they would fit right in with what I do with my students. I am only one teacher with over a hundred students, so I am stretched quite thin when it comes to time with each student. Having mentors for my students sounded like a dream come true, and publishing their stories in a book was a bonus. I especially liked the fact that the students would decide the theme of the book, and that they would have a say in every step of the process, because I knew that it would give them a strong sense of empowerment. At the beginning of the semester, I had a conversation with the students about the book. Together, they came up with the idea of hope as the central theme of the book and felt very strongly about wanting to show younger children who are living the lives they lived to see that they, too, can overcome troubles in their lives in order to realize the dream of graduating from a high school in the United States. They also wanted to change the world's perception of them, to smash every stereotype around. They wanted to tell their stories.

We began with a guided imagery exercise, during which Alli led the students in imagining what a perfect day would be like in ten years. I watched as some eagerly shared their dreams of looking at the moon out of a picture window, of being in control of their own lives, of being happy and free. Others teared up, unable to speak about what they had seen. One student wouldn't write anything down and cried when he finally confessed that he was afraid to write down his hope because he would be too crushed if things didn't, as usual, go well for him.

There were, of course, some bumps along the road. One student was angry, and felt that Alli was "just another white lady coming to save the bad kids" and was indignant because he thought that she had chosen us because we are not from a "good" neighborhood. He changed his mind quite quickly after meeting Alli, however. We had some trouble with technology, but that was sorted out when mentors generously donated flash drives for the students. Some students had internal struggles that their mentors helped resolve.

After the first meeting with the mentors, the students had only positive things to say. They were amazed that adults from other parts of town actually listened to them openly and without judgment. The students met with the mentors every Tuesday and Thursday during our regular class periods. On Mondays and Wednesdays I reinforced writing techniques. Alli provided me with some valuable materials for the students about the writing process from 826 Valencia. The most eye-opening for the students were copies of real authors' drafts. They understood that even published writers don't start with a pristine, perfect first draft, and this motivated them to keep revising and editing their own pieces.

The mentors seemed taken with the students right away and were even eager to help with more than just the project. One student was given a sewing machine to foster her talent in fashion design. Other mentors found scholarship information for their mentees or recommended books for them to read. Little gifts were exchanged, and the students became attached to their mentors. We all found ourselves looking forward to Tuesdays and Thursdays, and there was a palpable sense of disappointment when the first Tuesday without mentors arrived.

I noticed some changes in the students as well. Their confidence grew, as did their sense of identity. They became more goal-oriented and started talking about actually realizing their dreams instead of referring to them as just possibilities. After the writing process was done, we met with Watie White, the artist who was going to do the cover for our book. The students had amazing discussions with him and were not shy about sharing their ideas. As I watched and listened to them interact with him, I realized that this was not the same group of students I had started with. They knew their ideas were good. Here was a person they had never met before, and they trusted him right away not to judge them. And they didn't judge him, either. They spoke in terms of what they wanted people to see and think when they first saw the book. They were proud of their work and their progress, and they were sure of their work as worthy of a large audience.

I am so proud of my students, not only because they have written this book, but also because they are some of the bravest people that I know. They have overcome great odds and will graduate from high school, most as the first graduates in their families. I know that they will go on to create change in their communities and make their neighborhoods better places for generations to come.

One of my heroes, an amazing educator named Paolo Freire, in his book *Pedagogy of Freedom* stated that,

> "It's impossible to talk of respect for students for the dignity that is in the process of coming to be, for the identities that are in the process of construction, without taking into con sideration the conditions in which they are living and the importance of the knowledge derived from life experience, which they bring with them to school. I can in no way underestimate such knowledge. Or what is worse, ridicule it" (p. 62).

This project has shown my students Freire's kind of respect. The students felt safe bringing their lives into discussion with the mentors and with me, and in doing so, without them even realizing it, they learned so much: the writing process, the publishing process, responsibility, team work, cooperation, trust, and respect. They stopped judging others and expecting judgment in return. I am certain that the mentors took just as much away from the project as my students did.

In the same book, Freire says, "The absence of hope is not the "normal" way to be human" (p.69). The Omaha Young Writers Project showed my students how to hope.

Reference

Freire, P. (1998). *Pedagogy of Freedom: Ethics, Democracy, and Civic Courage*. Lanham, MD: Rowman & Littlefield Publishers Inc.

Epilogue
How Every Adult and Community
Can Spread Hope

by Shane J. Lopez, Ph.D.
Senior Scientist in Residence, Gallup
Research Director, Clifton Strengths School
Mentor, The Omaha Young Writers Project

My students at Omaha South High School don't want to be rappers or professional athletes. They want what all of us want—a good job and someone to love. If all goes well, Cody will be a barber and business owner, Erica will be a helper, maybe a teacher or nurse, Juan will be a physical therapist and Victor will be Omaha's best mechanic. And all of them will be surrounded by friends and family.

Discussions of students' current realities were sometimes as depressing as the chats about the students' dreams were exhilarating. Student after student told stories about the biggest obstacles in their lives. Over a couple of mentoring sessions, I realized that all four of my students were talking about a common obstacle: us, the adults in their lives who are responsible for their care, learning and growth.

I believe that every adult and every community has the responsibility of making kids' lives better. To do so, each adult needs to be hopeful and each community needs to knock down the obstacles that keep our youth stuck.

Making the Case for Hope

Hopeful students see the future as better than the present and believe they have the power to make it so. Hope—the ideas and energy for the future—is one of the most potent predictors of success of our youth.

Scientists from around the world have studied hope in kids, and this is what we know: Hopeful students are energetic, full of life. They are able to develop many strategies to reach goals and plan contingencies in the event that they are faced with problems along the way. Hopeful middle school students have better grades in core subjects and higher scores on achievement tests. Hopeful high school students and beginning college students have higher overall grade point averages. In numerous studies, the predictive power of hope remained significant, even when controlling for intelligence, prior grades, self-esteem and college entrance examination scores such as high school GPA and ACT/SAT.

The twenty years of field research demonstrates that more hopeful students do better in school and life than less hopeful students. Over the last 10 years, through study after study, I have demonstrated that hope is malleable, that the hopeless can learn to be hopeful and, unfortunately, that we can strip hope away from one another. Our youth need a focused effort from us, the people who care about them and their future, to build their hope and to buffer them from the people who want to take it away.

Spreading Hope Throughout Schools and Communities

All adults can assume a role in spreading hope throughout a school and communities by (1) creating excitement about the future, (2) teaching numerous strategies for solving problems and (3) knocking down obstacles.

Create excitement about the future. Big goals get people excited and bring them together. On a local level, communities race for the cure, plant neighborhood gardens, and raise money for their favorite charities. Unfortunately, people inside and outside of the four walls of a school don't get very excited about raising math, reading, and science scores, studying for the ACT/SAT, or writing college essays. American students themselves, though confident that they will graduate school and one day get a good job, have little energy and excitement for their big goals. Based on findings from a representative sample of students completing the Gallup Student Poll, only 4 in 10 students energetically pursue their goals.

Getting people excited about the future requires setting a goal that is emotionally important to people young and old, tracking the progress toward that goal in a visual way, and celebrating the progress and/or the attainment of the goal. The focus of a prosocial goal only matters to the extent it excites people and progress can be marked.

Regarding everyday behaviors, adults can tweak their formal and informal communication so that it inspires young people rather than frustrates them. Hopeful communication can make others enthusiastic about the future, or communication can undermine the excitement that others feel about their day, week, or even their school year. Speeches, classroom teaching, parent teacher conferences, phone calls, letters, emails, Facebook updates, tweets, and text messages need to say what is intended and, when possible, need to communicate excitement about the future and wishes for others. More simply, each casual interaction an adult has with a kid should communicate joy and interest.

Teach the "ways" to solve problems. Students generally have the will to pursue a future they desire, but they lack the ways or necessary strategies to reach the big goals of graduation and employment. For example, in Gallup's representative survey of students, nearly half of American students strongly believed that they will find a good job after graduation but only a third of them (35%) strongly believed that they can find ways around any problem that might arise in life.

Given the intense commitment to teaching and learning academic content in each class during each school day, the process of solving daily problems may remain a mystery. Student hope may be enhanced by small efforts to teach them the ways to study for tests, prepare for the examination period, track grades over time, solve small interpersonal disputes, pursue career interests, interview for jobs, etc.

Knocking down obstacles. In our most hopeful neighborhoods, community members proactively help the school create a desirable future for the students. Knocking down obstacles to students' big goals shows (rather than tells) the community how to make hope happen beyond the walls of the school.

Communities can't knock down obstacles until they know what they are…and students will tell you with little prodding. So, how about meeting with local students to identify the top ten obstacles to success at school and happiness in life? Behavioral rules that no longer serve the function will no doubt top the list of barriers to the future. Physical obstacles to getting to school also might be high on the list. Once you have a working list, then obstacles can be addressed one by one.

Many obstacles pop up and threaten the development of students, but the students who have both the will and the ways are most likely to reach their goals.

Back to Omaha South High School. The Omaha Young Writers Project mentors and students spent 11 class periods together. The project and the mentors helped students turn excitement about ideas into provocative essays. More importantly, the project gave the students a voice, and encouraged them to be bold in the pursuit of their own ideas. Over time, it became clear that the students began to use that voice to tell a story about how they would make the future better than the present.

About the Authors

As the six weeks of tutoring sessions drew to a close, the writing mentors decided to write bios about the students to show them how much we were paying attention to them. While this was originally intended as merely a fun and supportive exercise, the students decided to use them here, which may be just as well because perhaps they would be too modest in describing themselves.

Hugo Alvarez takes little for granted. He wisely knows he's been extremely fortunate because others believe in him. In his friendly, personable manner, he expresses appreciation often and sincerely. To Hugo, hard work is routine - on the soccer field, in school and on the job. Good natured and driven, Hugo admirably longs to share his optimism for a bright future by giving young children support and opportunity to find their gifts and realize their potential.

Brad Arnold's writing is like paint strokes on a page – quick, thoughtful, flowing. He is already a talented artist and has a clear focus about the kind of work he will be doing in the future. His natural eye for detail allows him to create beauty out of common objects or transform a blank canvas. Art is life for Brad.

Juan Ayala is a first generation American who says he had the gift of a "better future" given to him by his parents. His writing reflects his family history and his hopes and dreams for the days and years to come. Juan balances his love for basketball with the discipline needed to complete his studies so that he can take advantage of the sacrifices his parents have made for him. He is a gentle soul who speaks with a quiet voice, but his heart is that of a lion.

Pamela M. Blanco's ideas and writing flow like a river of knowledge called Memories. She is a mature young woman who has already gained wisdom through experiences in her life. Her love for her family is where she finds strength. Pamela's eyes shine with hope when she talks about accomplishing her goals of gaining an education and finding success in the United States.

Salimah Buhari is an inspiration. Despite her youth, she is undeniably comfortable with who she is: genuine, funny, good-natured and well-grounded. Though she has known pain, she eagerly faces a future of her own making. Original in her thinking, she skillfully expresses her vision to stay true to herself.

Erica Brown is the star in her everyday comedy and drama. She is passionate about her Jordans and about her future. In the fall of 2010, she will be attending college at the University of Nebraska-Omaha.

Maira Camarillo is one of those people with a contagious smile and a peaceful spirit; she is the type of person that everyone likes to be around. It is clear that Maira's priorities are her family and friends; she is a definite people person. She writes from her soul, which results in beautiful and moving prose.

Daniella Chavez's strong love and deep respect for her family pours from her heart through her writing. She's an exceptionally bright and positive young woman, who has gained strength and uncommon insight through both adverse and positive experiences she has faced in her young life. There's a luminosity that shines when she writes of hopes for owning a business with her mother, and there is no doubt that with the continued support of her loving family, absolutely nothing will stand in the way of Daniella reaching her goals.

Alex De la Rocha is an amazing individual who is looking forward to connecting in his interests in mixed martial arts and his love for cooking. He is considering a career in the marines. His close relationship with his family can inspire us all.

Shy **Agustina Degante-Cambray** is not to be underestimated. Her concern for the rights of immigrants runs deep. Naturally cautious, she takes time to express herself. Yet, her conviction is fierce. The intensity of her compassion creates a quiet power, which adversaries of justice would be wise not to disregard.

Kody Deleon is a true artist. Though young, he has very sophisticated insights into the artistic process, and he understands the vast possibilities for the reach and influence of visual art. We have much to learn from Kody about the power of personal expression.

Monica Diego is very good at exploring her past and expressing her thoughts on what she's experienced and how these experiences are driving her desires for her own child. It's clear that Monica has big dreams for her son, and it's exciting to read and discuss all the possibilities she is envisioning for him, as well as for herself.

Dominique Dominguez writes as she speaks, as a storyteller of truths. She serves up her story with a directness that resembles the stories grandmothers must have told around hot stoves in winter. Dominique approaches life with a similar straightforward nature by righting that which is wrong and moving on to a future full of new stories.

A bounty of enthusiasm rings in **Joslynn Galvan's** voice. A proud young mother, she envisions a better life for her son. What she lacks in confidence, she makes up for in passion. Her dream of becoming a delivery room nurse is not free of obstacles. yet the depth of her passion to help others and the intense love for her son strengthen her will.

Maria Garcia has received an education about life that only comes through experience. A true cadet, she realizes what it's like to be a part of something bigger than yourself. Maria has developed the ability to think logically (she has both a plan and a back-up plan for her future), and her ability to communicate is as also well- developed. Her essay will inspire!

Angel Gomez's hope for the future is driven by his heartfelt desire to create beauty and share it with others. A genuinely gifted artist, he maintains a refreshingly humble attitude regarding his remarkable talent. Angel constantly pursues the improvement of his already advanced skills – all for the sake of realizing his dream to one-day create masterpieces that will be cherished for a lifetime.

Gerardo Gonzalez gives fully of himself to the reader. As he offers up the truths of his mind and his heart, he invites the reader to understand their own truths. Gerardo writes with his senses, giving the reader the entirety of his experience through his nose, his mouth, his eyes, and his ears. His self-awareness, observance of his surroundings, and knowledge of right and wrong will continue to build him into a great man.

Santiago Gonzalez' physical strength—though impressive—is nothing compared to his mental strength. As a power lifter, he is in charge of his own destiny. The same is true for his writing. If Santiago flexes his pen as though it were his muscle, he will deliver.

Michael Gray has a strong sense of family and of the importance of family history. From his experiences, he draws creativity and artistic invention. Among his gifts is the ability to take personal experience and allow it to feed his imagination and shape his talent.

Martell Harris' writing shows his connectedness to his family and friends. He shares rich details with the reader: one can almost taste his mom's spaghetti sauce or see his grandfather slipping him a couple of Lincolns for a night out. This project forced Martell to explore of the specifics of his career goal of becoming a coach or athletic trainer.

Natividad "Naty" Hernandez is the epitome of courage and hope. She is an incredible storyteller and writer. She finds her strength in her family and in her future where she foresees herself as a caretaker and mother. When she speaks of hope and her love of life, you couldn't imagine anything more inspiring.

Ruben Jaime has a dream that someday everyone will see past color and live in harmony. His writing is bursting with enthusiasm for his hope that one day there will be no racism in the world. He coaches soccer for young kids and spending time with them is a reminder to him that little kids don't discriminate based on race. Ruben enjoys giving something back to his community and makes a difference by leading through example.

Victor Lopez has a quiet wisdom borne out of a trying past and a deep desire to build a brighter future. A natural entrepreneur, he has built a small business giving new life to old cars. He aims to own his own auto repair shop and be the best he can be in life.

Juan Martinez moved to Nebraska when he was six years old. He chases the American dream on the soccer field and in the classroom. In the fall of 2010, he will take his skills to college, where he will play soccer and major in physical therapy.

Merissa Martinez seeks the good in everyone. She understands the struggles others, which comes from experiences in her own life. Merissa's unique way of writing exudes strength and she chooses words carefully because she knows they are meaningful. As a strong woman, Merissa is a beautifully reflective.

Cars. Plain and simple. **Travis Masilko's** existence revolves around cars. As long as he can remember, he has enjoyed tinkering with engines and does not mind getting his hands nice and filthy. Farsighted, Travis realizes he needs more computerized auto training through MCC or another community college to reach his goal of opening his own auto repair shop.

Duol Mayot may sport a calm demeanor, but there is no mistaking his passion for basketball when he starts writing. Readers may feel compelled to pick up a basketball for the first time after reading Duol's work. It quickly becomes clear to readers that this smart young man has already lived more than many adults have lived. His writing is honest, open, and intriguing.

Eric Morgan has a strong, positive moral code and work ethic. He is open to suggestions and definitely profits from mishaps. His recollection of grandparental persuasion is phenomenal, and he definitely writes with a creative flair. He dreams of flying and sometimes wears a sharp black vest.

You have got to appreciate the fohawk; way to rock good hair. **Pedro Muñoz** struggled in the middle of this project with some real human issues—the kind that we all must make sense of at different times in our adult lives. Pedro made his mentor proud by pushing through in a positive way.

Abel Nava is so curious and interested in everything. It is clear that Abel cares very much for his family and it shows in his writing. Abel is a strong writer and he has the stamina to sit down and write his thoughts down in a very fluid way. It shows in his writing that Abel writes in the same pattern as his thinking process and this works for his story. He writes just enough to tell what's happening without clouding his story with too many ideas.

Susana Ornelas has done the rarest of human things; she has learned from her mistakes and changed the course of her life. She plans to recruit her two sisters to enroll in college with her so that they can attend together. She is currently an honor roll student, and she is considering a career in either communications or a profession through which she help other people.

Jesse Ortiz is filled with a vibrancy and energy that he puts into every word of his writing. An old soul in a young man's body, Jesse's life experiences and his overcoming of great obstacles have fueled a fire deep inside that burns bright with his desire for success. Evident through his poetry and writing, Jesse is armed with a passion for achievement and a sense of maturity that most his age will never know. Jesse has the courage, attitude and determination to be a positive influence in this world, and his triumph in everything he sets his mind to is certain.

Jenifer Perez has the courage and imagination to pursue all the great opportunities destined to come her way. Her love for poetry and music give her an artist's perspective and a powerfully unique vision.

Pedro Perez has an old soul. His writing reflects his speech and in it you can feel the love he has for his family. He found light in the form of his baby sister during a dark time in his family's life. He is unaware that this same light shines from within him.

Elias Placido displays a strong sense of security rooted in his Spring Lake neighborhood, his family and their frequent trips to Mexico. Either on his Huffy bike or in the back of an SUV bound for the border, Elias personifies a "man on the move."

Desirae Priebe is prepared to knock down any obstacle that gets in her way. She is poised to succeed and is willing to work hard in order to reach her goals. Her writing is touching and peppered with imagery that allows the reader to better understand the Desirae as a writer, student, and lovely young lady.

Erica Ramos' belief in true love and honest forgiveness is expressed in words that draw the reader into her world. Her compassion for those who have failed her gives the reader the opportunity to ask for their own forgiveness. She is an engaging young woman who will continue to share her beauty and confidence with everyone in her future.

Alexis Reyes is a caring, bright young woman whose writing is progressing as she is finding her voice and story. She has already discovered how to use tough circumstances as motivation – a trait that will serve her well in life. Though she's quiet, her eyes and her smile reveal the goodness that is inside her.

Maria "Sammy" Sinecio shows so much determination in her life and it is reflected in her written story. She has seen incredibly unsettling things and her family has experienced much pain, but she has turned these things into motivation to do something positive. Sammy has a desire to make her community, and the world, a better place and she knows exactly what she needs to do to reach her goals. Her drive and focus is sure to be an inspiration to many.

Rachel Skarda, the girl with the gorgeous, smoky eyes and soft, scrunched hair, explodes with pen and paper, finding herself in her own written words. She sometimes judges herself harshly but has the brainpower to do just about whatever, and once she finds her "whatever" during her post-high school education, nothing will stop her from succeeding.

Aubri Starks is a young woman with an abundance of spirit and a focus on the future. She knows that she controls her own destiny. It is only a matter of time before she goes off on her own and becomes the woman she sees in the mirror.

Rayna Ursdevenicz is learning to look to the future and dreams of a life that is ordered and peaceful. She is an aspiring designer and would like to attend the Kansas City Art Institute. She plays soccer, is very talented at sewing and has a new puppy.

Shay Valentine is thoughtful and fun, reflective and confident, curious and caring. She is a person that makes everyone around her better. Her unparalleled openness to new experiences and the courageous way she continually challenges herself to grow will undoubtedly take her to fascinating places.

Sarah Valles' writing is authentic and frank. Behind that authenticity of voice lies an inquisitive mind and cheeky intelligence. If you are lucky, Sarah involves you in her trifecta of creativity: art, music and dance, and you are delighted with her poise, courage, and openheartedness.

Cody Woodruff has a deep and resonant soul. His quiet power attracts others and propels him forward. After graduating, he will attend barber college in the fall of 2010 and hopes to one day own a barber shop. He would like to have a family and move to a bigger city on a coast, such as Los Angeles or Miami.

About the Cover

Every part of this book was shaped by the student writers, from the choice of the theme at the very beginning to the content and message of the cover artwork. Before he began developing the images for the covers, artist Watie White met with the students to discuss the overall message they were trying to send with the book. He explained that the cover is not only a representation of the book's contents; it's also the first story of the book that a potential reader will see. He invited the students to talk about what the title *In My Shoes* meant to them and how they wanted to be understood. The student suggestions began with the obvious—shoes—and then moved into more complex ideas for images that convey how it feels to be a teenager, to feel vulnerable and to feel judged without being truly known or understood.

The result of those discussions is the cover art. In the images, which feature two student writers as models, each student looks into a mirror but doesn't see himself looking back; he sees someone else. Their shirtlessness conveys their sense of vulnerability, and the labels slapped on their backs represent the kind of judgments they and their friends feel are cast against kids like them every day. The labels were provided by the two students, who shared troublesome words and ideas that they have encountered. While the contents of the book convey that their words have power, the title and cover art convey another truth: words can hurt, too.

Acknowledgments

The 45 student writers who shared their stories to create this book.

Ferial Pearson, for being a great partner teacher in this project and for creating an emotional environment in your classroom that makes even the most guarded students feel safe, respected and valued.

The writing mentors—Bruce Arant, Steve Brock, Tamsen Butler, Amy Chittenden, Cynthia English, Shelley Erikson, Amanda Ferrell, Dan Gilbert, Emilio Herrera, Shane Lopez, Ali Maloy, William Meinen, Summer Miller, Jessica Mogis, JerLene Mosley, Dave Mullens, Suszi Munson, Nancy Novak, Natalie Petersen and Natalie Peterson (AKA the Natalies), Marty Pierson, Katie Knapp Schubert, Timothy Schaffert, Jill Siciliano, Sarah Skarka, Lori Umstead, Liz Varela and Trilety Wade—for answering the call for volunteers, for giving of your time and of yourselves to these students and for rearranging your lives to be a part of this project. You turned this idea into a reality.

Assistant editors Sarah Skarka, Liz Varela, Tamsen Butler and Shane Lopez for helping with proofreading and editing with the intent of respecting and preserving the students' unique voices.

Liz Varela for suggesting that the writing mentors write bios of their students and for collecting and organizing that task.

Jesse Ortiz for sharing your poem "1,000 Miles" and for allowing me to include it in the introduction.

Watie White for beautiful cover art and for engaging the students in great discussions about how the right cover image is a visual metaphor to draw readers to their book. Thank you for honoring them with your talents.

Oliva Rodriguez, our student photographer, for taking the student head shots.

Cara Riggs, principal of Omaha South High Magnet School, for your initial excitement, unwavering support and genuine passion for what you do. Every student should have a principal like you leading their school. You are love and respect walking down those halls.

Shelley Erikson, supervisor of English, language arts and reading at the Omaha Public School District, for your enthusiasm, advocacy and introduction to Principal Riggs. I asked you for a superstar teacher, a welcoming school and a dynamic principal who would support us, and you surpassed my hopes. And having you join us as one of our writing mentors was a great bonus.

Omaha Public Schools Superintendent John Mackiel for enthusiasm and support.

The Gallup Education Division for donating office supplies.

The Sherwood Foundation for supporting the book printing and book release party, as well as for generously sending a cohort of 24 Omaha educators to the Freedom Writers Institute in summer 2010, which helped to establish a great foundation for this project. Your efforts on behalf of students in Omaha and beyond are inspirational. Thank you for existing. Thanks to Jerry

Bexton for coordinating our experience and supporting this project.

Erin Gruwell and the staff at the Freedom Writers Foundation for writing the foreword for the book and for an amazing experience in Long Beach, for inspiration and for the fierce conviction that a passionate and caring person can make a difference in the lives of kids.

Erin Archuleta at 826 National for advice on planning an in-school book project.

Dave Eggers for giving the TED Talk that inspired this project.

Connie Clifton Rath, Cheryl Beamer and Nancy Oberst for acting as board members and fairy godmothers to this project.

Timothy Schaffert and Rodney Dahl of the (Downtown) Omaha Lit Fest for acting as our 501c3 steward.

Shane J. Lopez, the leading researcher on hope, for guidance in structuring introductory activities with the students to provoke hope and for passionate support at every stage of the project.

Cindy Grady and WriteLife, LLC Publishing for helping to shepherd this book out to the world.

You, the reader, for taking the time to listen to the voice of American teenagers and for considering what they have to say. May this be the first of many times you do this, because they need it so much.